THE SECRET
LANGUAGE OF

THE SECRET LANGUAGE OF

How to Tell Visual Stories with Data

Carissa Carter

Illustrations by Jeremy Nguyen & Michael Hirshon

TEN SPEED PRESS
California | New York

HASSO PLATTNER
Institute of Design at Stanford

Contents

Murder, She Mapped
A Mystery Story

A Note from the d.school

At the Stanford d.school, *design* is a verb. It's an attitude to embody and a way to work. The core of that work is trying, to the best of one's abilities, to help things run more smoothly, delight more people, and ease more suffering. This holds true for you, too—whether design is your profession or simply a mindset you bring to life.

Founded in 2005 as a home for wayward thinkers, the d.school was a place where independent-minded people could gather, try out ideas, and make change. A lot has shifted in the decade or so since, but that original exuberant and resourceful attitude is as present today as it was then.

Our series of guides is here to offer you the same inventiveness, insight, optimism, and perseverance that we champion at the d.school. Like a good tour guide, these handbooks will help you find your way through unknown territory and introduce you to some fundamental ideas that we hope will become cornerstones in your creative foundation.

Learn to build inclusive communities in *Design for Belonging*. Uncover surprising opportunities in *Navigating Ambiguity*. And in this book, learn how to decode hidden meaning and tell compelling stories with data.

Welcome to *The Secret Language of Maps*!

love,
the d.school

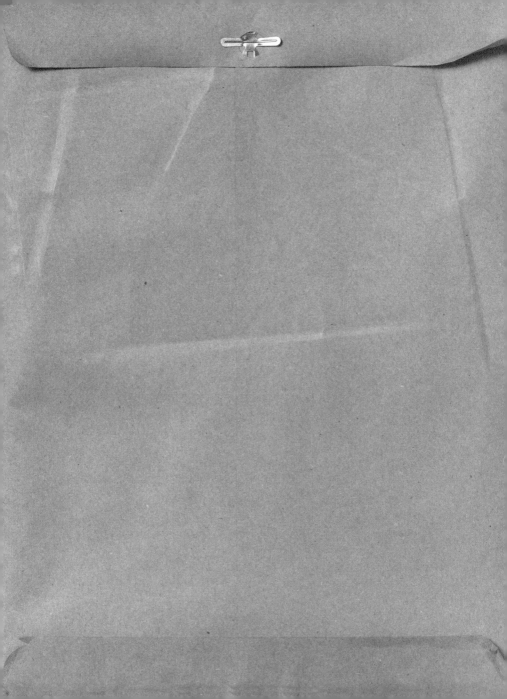

The Investigation

Take it apart to figure out how it works.

Murder, She Mapped
A Mystery Story

CHAPTER I

Marion Marlow wondered if the giant plastic fish hook slung over the left side of her lower lip enjoyed sucking every bit of moisture from her mouth. It was tethering her to the moment through the symphony of dental care.

Where do you look when you're at the dentist? Do you stare at the roof? Close your eyes? Follow the creases in the assistant's face? When you're wearing the suction, are you supposed to keep up a conversation?

Marion tested three landing points for her eyes, then let them settle on the masked face of Emily Romero. Twenty-five years before, Emily was just the crazy younger sister of Marion's best friend, Julie. Emily skipped class, blew cigarette smoke at smoke detectors, and spent most of 1995 sitting on bumpers in the parking lot of Burke High School, talking about Kurt Cobain.

Now Dr. Emily Romero suggested that Marion close her eyes and "just relax while I'm polishing."

It was supposed to be me, thought Marion. *Me or Julie. The older girls. The ones who tried. We were the ones destined to be the world-savers. Or at least we'd be the lawyers, the professors, the presidents, the ones envied by everyone for their achievements . . . the dentists.* Back then, she'd never considered the possibility that she might not win in life. But at this point in her life she hadn't even earned a participation ribbon. *Should I ask about Julie? Would Emily want to talk about her? Should I sound casual or concerned? Does Emily blame me?* It'd been so long since the day that Julie had disappeared.

◆ ◆ ◆

◆ *January 1996* ◆

Marion and Julie were both home in New England for the holiday break from their first year of college. Those were lonely times. Neither one had made a friend in college who lived up to the standard they'd each set for the other. Julie should have studied history or poetry and surrounded herself with books and been an academic, but impractical wasn't in her budget. She slogged through a semester of business classes and arrived home on break ready to retire. Marion had the luxury of choice but was as awkward as an aardvark in the ocean. She didn't know how to fit in—she always felt like she was treading water outside of the real conversations. Julie had always been her raft.

On January 6, 1996, just after 11 p.m., Julie and Marion cut through the snowy woods to their old high school. The door by the smokers' corner could always be opened with a Swiss Army knife. There was no deadbolt; just slide the blade between the double doors and depress the lock. It would always pull open.

The halls smelled the same—a mix of that shiny textbook paper and potato chips. Sitting next to the D-block lockers, they were back in the nest.

A set of keys hit the ground way down the hall. Someone backed out of the teachers' lounge and pulled the door shut. The person pivoted right toward Marion and Julie, then stared at them for a breath. On the inhale the person started to run right toward them. Marion and Julie froze in place on the linoleum. No fight-or-flight instincts materialized. Marion was sure they'd been caught.

The gust of air from the runner's draft smelled like cold air and exercise. The runner was all in black, a knit mask and boots, an envelope under one arm, steps quick, gaze unwavering.

Julie and Marion remained immobilized until the smokers' door slammed. Then they mimed a swift agreement to follow the runner. They rushed downstairs and saw the dark figure disappear down the same path they'd taken from the snowy woods.

◆ ◆ ◆

They argued all week about what to do. Marion wanted to tell someone about the school intruder. She insisted that the school couldn't kick them out—they'd already graduated. Julie said no way—she didn't want to get in trouble, become a police blotter item for trespassing. "Besides," Julie said, "we don't even know if anything was stolen. It could have been a teacher." She pleaded with Marion not to tell a soul.

And that was it. It felt odd to Marion that Julie didn't want to do what Marion was sure was the right thing, but Marion agreed, reluctantly. She went back to college a few days before Julie was set to return. They were on mildly grumpy terms.

Marion would never hear from Julie again.

Unanswered calls. Letters. Emails. Julie had vanished. She never returned to college. Everyone was interviewed. Her home was searched. No leads, no evidence of foul play, and no Julie.

Later that January, a literary magazine published an essay by Julie. Initially everyone thought this meant she was alive but wished to remain away. Further investigation revealed that she sent in her submission over the winter break, before she disappeared.

Julie was gone, probably dead, they told Marion.

"Julie would want you to pursue your dreams."

"Julie would want you to go for it. To accomplish something."

"Julie would want you to keep moving."

They said a lot of things. But how do you find your footing again after a best friend leaves you without warning?

After college, Marion stayed in California through a series of jobs, never finding one that held her interest. And her employers weren't ever particularly interested in her, either. It wasn't a life she could be proud of.

◆ ◆ ◆

Emily straightened up and pulled down her surgical mask. "Done. And the filling fix is on me."

"Oh no. That's crazy . . . thank you, though." Marion was relieved she wouldn't have to pay.

Emily stood and stared at Marion, still supine and bibbed. She raised the back of the dental chair, bringing Marion to an upright position, but gestured for her to stay put. Emily looked like she was about to say something. Marion waited. Emily opened her mouth. "I—" But the words didn't come. She looked down for a second, then stared at a photograph of snowy woods hanging on the wall. Marion followed her gaze to the picture. It was familiar. Local. Then Emily walked over and lifted it off its hook. She put the large frame facedown on the counter and unclipped the metal strips holding the cardboard backing. She lifted it out and set it aside.

Marion was as rigid as she'd been on that January night in 1996. She watched Emily lift five items out from behind the picture. Emily placed these, along with the snowy woods photo, in a manila folder. She handed the folder to Marion, but didn't let go of it or break eye contact. "I know this is all about Julie. I need you to find her."

← Ochre mine

berry show

BY JULIE ROMERO

They're maples, but not the kind that will bring syrup. We four students walk out into the woods beyond the black...

The best kind of smoke is...up today. It's mismatc... but doesn't reso... tent. We clinch... Turlock at the... electric orange... pristine and... She fixes me... and I...

Seasons
are
Senses

spring

Summer

Some things
are really unhealthy!

26.75

15

10

5

71° 15'
42° 30'

BER...
GE...

69 III SE

47 07 000m N

× 287
• Water Tank

WILSON

47 06

PIPE ROAD

200

3.25

3.625

7

UNITED STATES
DEPARTMENT OF THE INTERIOR
GEOLOGICAL SURVEY

What is a map?

◀ Is this a map?

You can't get this one wrong. Is it a map? Yes. How do we know? It has buildings, roads, a north symbol. It describes a place. This map might help us understand what happens in this place. It's what most of us think of when we think *map*. It's a useful starting point. The crux of what makes the geographic map a map is that its elements are related spatially and presented visually—they just happen to be depicting a geography.

▼ How about this? Is this a map?

BY JULIE ROMERO

They're maples, but not the kind that will bring syrup. We four students walk out into the woods beyond the blacktop. The best kind of snow showed up today. It's massively fluffy but doesn't crest my moon boot. We circle around Ms. Turlock as she sprinkles the electric orange powder on a pristine square foot of snow. She passes around the spoon and all four of us eat the delicacy that is Tang plus snow.

Being in snowy woods is a specific feeling. The quiet is heavy. The body is hot. The breath is big. You don't have to go too far to find it. Fifty feet in?

This forest is accommodating in the winter. It no longer forces you onto its paths. It welcomes you from any direction to any destination. It allows you to see and navigate for yourself, no longer reliant on the guidance of someone else's trail. You become visible too. Enveloped but exposed, aware but naive. But what is your purpose? Are you here just to feel? These woods are a refuge but offer a different kind of haven in winter than in spring. In spring, the forest is in charge. Its paths, its insects, its poison ivy. We are allowed to pass through, but on the terms of the environment. If each season has a sense, smell belongs to spring. Freshness cracks through. New sprouts, new blooms cut through last year's layer of composting leaves. Summer is for sticky touch. Fall is for sound. The crunch is deafening. Crispy oak, maple, and birch intertwine underfoot. But, winter. Winter is about a sixth sense. It's the only one where you are in charge.

No, a story is not a map. But you could map a story. If the above story was a map, it might look like the drawing on the right. Or a story could be mapped like the drawing on the next page.

winter

fall

spring

summer

Seasons
are
Senses

← Ochee
mine

berry
shrubs

school

her woods

yearly
burn-out

Last
Stand

Tang
spot

black-top

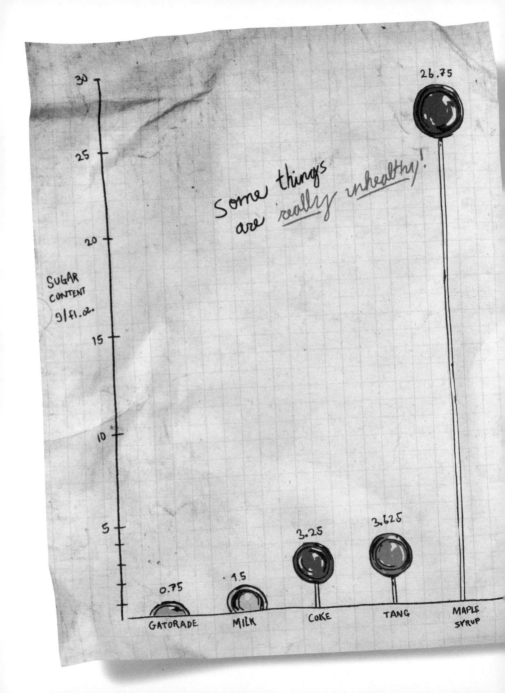

A map might also look like the chart on the left.

These are all maps. They show spatial relationships in a visual way. They aren't all geographic, but they are still maps.

In this book, "map" is a bucket term for information that's sorted spatially and depicted (even slightly) visually. This includes infographics and frameworks. Many different maps can describe the same experience. Making maps gives us a chance to slice the same concept, the same data, in multiple ways. Maps allow us to focus on different aspects of a scenario and reveal them to our viewer in our own way.

▾ How about this?

Not a map. A photograph is a snapshot of a moment in time. In a map, the components within it need to be organized in relationship to one another. Maps utilize the placement of information on a page. They are always one or more degrees abstracted from reality.

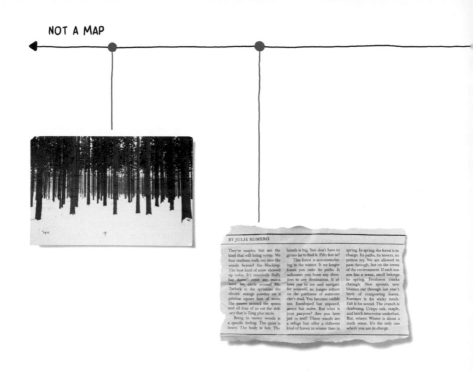

BY JULIE ROMERO

They're maples, but not the kind that will bring syrup. We four students walk out into the woods beyond the blacktop. The best kind of snow showed up today. It's massively fluffy but doesn't crest my mono boot. We circle around Mt. Turlock as she sprinkles the electric orange powder on a pristine square foot of snow. She passes around the spoon and all four of us eat the delicacy that is Tang plus snow.

Being in snowy woods is a specific feeling. The quiet is heavy. The body is hot. The breath is big. You don't have to go too far to find it. Fifty feet in?

This forest is accommodating in the winter. It no longer forces you onto its paths. It welcomes you from any direction to any destination. It allows you to see and navigate for yourself, no longer reliant on the guidance of someone else's trail. You become visible too. Enveloped but exposed, aware but naïve. But what is your purpose? Are you here just to feel? These woods are a refuge but offer a different kind of haven in winter than in

spring. In spring, the forest is in charge. Its paths, its insects, its poison ivy. We are allowed to pass through, but on the terms of the environment. If each season has a sense, smell belongs to spring. Freshness cracks through. New sprouts, new blooms cut through last year's layer of composting leaves. Summer is for sticky touch. Fall is for sound. The crunch is deafening. Crispy oak, maple, and birch intertwine underfoot. But, winter. Winter is about a sixth sense. It's the only one where you are in charge.

⋀ Finally, what about this one?

Yes! It's a map about what a map is. It's a meta map. Actually, it's its own kind of map—a continuum. A continuum is a line with two arrows. It is the most elegant and simple of all maps. Continua help us sort, express, and discover information. They can highlight almost anything: timelines, either/ors, descriptions of from-this-to-that, things that smell gross to things that smell sweet, and so much more. There are many qualities and uses that apply to many disciplines with the humble continuum.

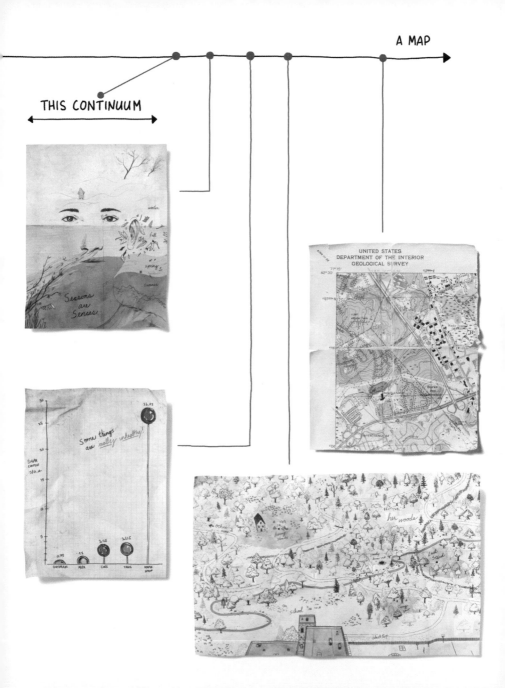

A MAP

THIS CONTINUUM

So, what's a map?

Maps can be geographic. They can be infographic. They might be based on real places, experiences, or data. They might be completely fictitious. Sometimes they're used to explain or present a scenario, polished with a point of view. Other times they are scratch paper—frameworks used to investigate or uncover new ideas. Maps harbor and expose our assumptions. They allow us to mark what we think is obvious and what is obfuscated, what is noticed and what is hidden.

Maps might tell you where to go. They might show you what you already know. They could uncover phenomena you had no idea existed. Sometimes people use them to do things that are a little bit twisted. You can use maps to look for patterns and _____.* If a topic is so dense that you need a nap, you could try to find a new insight by making a map.

Maps are welcoming. They invite exploration. Maps don't assume truth. Or at least they shouldn't. Actually, every single map in the world is a combination of the real and the imaginary. Whether you intend to or not, when you create any map you create something that teeters on the make-believe.

But remember, the creator of the map doesn't hold all the power. Not at all! The map alone can't do everything. It brings the viewer to a certain point, a place to jump off from and react to, and then the viewer has to take it from there. Just as the mapmaker has their subjective perspective, every viewer has their own way of filling in the lines, their own biases and experiences that they unload on the map. Everyone will finish the map differently. Still, if you are the creator of a map, you have a great responsibility in how you set up the information for the viewer.

Bias, data, and craft

Deconstruct any map, and you will find an interplay between three components: bias, data, and craft. These exist in creative tension with each other. Be aware, and read them with care. They aren't always what they seem to be.

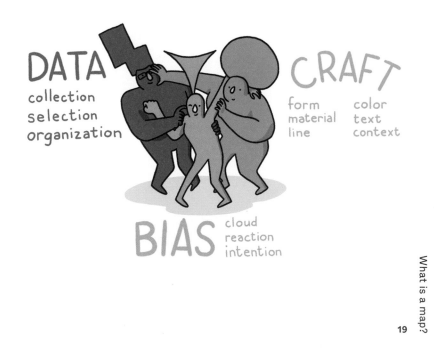

DATA
collection
selection
organization

CRAFT
form   color
material   text
line   context

BIAS   cloud
        reaction
        intention

Bias: We don't easily separate from ourselves.

As a human, you are loaded with biases. These biases are formed from your current life circumstances and your past experiences and culture. As you create a map, your biases are in constant tension with the data in your map and its visual design or craft. A map is a window into the worldview of its creator.

Biases might be implicit or explicit, intentional or unintentional. The creator might be trying to sway the viewer by presenting data in a specific way. Or they may have crafted a map specifically for one setting, but it could be used out of context and misinterpreted.

Data: Enough may or may not be enough.

Data is the information used to construct the map. Data can be quantitative, qualitative, or somewhere in between. How data is collected, how it's selected, and how it's organized—all these decisions are made by the mapmaker.

The data included in a map is as important as the data that's left out. There are many reasons why data might be left out. It might never have been noticed. The mapmaker might not have had the tools for capturing it. The data might have been so extreme that the mapmaker considered it an outlier. The mapmaker may have intentionally ignored it.

What tools were used to collect and record the data? Who was interviewed? Who wasn't? What's included, and what's omitted? It all makes a difference.

Craft: How it's made is what it means.

Craft is the visual design of the map. It's the lever that's easiest to ignore, to claim is unimportant, to outsource to stock chart makers in a spreadsheet application. It's also the easiest tool for setting the mood and conveying your point of view. Craft includes form, size, colors, captions, labels, and materials. Anything used in building the map has meaning. The same map drawn messily on scrap paper with a pencil will be interpreted very differently if printed in full color and displayed on a billboard.

Words are important. Their tone conveys your intent. Change a title from funny to serious, and you've changed the whole map. Leave out the title, and viewers need to interpret that intent for themselves. Have you included labels? Words and their placement are the maple drizzle that completes your dessert. Leave them out, and someone might put mayonnaise on top of your cake. Overuse them, and the sweetness is unbearable.

Intention in tension

Data, bias, and craft are individual elements that are perpetually intertwined. If you understand the tension between these elements, you can decipher intention. Understand how the parts work, and you can better figure out the point of the whole thing. It isn't simple. When everything is connected, you can't pull one string without affecting another. But you can explore the raw materials of each and watch as they tug on the map as a whole.

CHAPTER II

"I'll have a medium cap—" she started to say, beginning her order at the shop that used to be Coffee Connection.

"Marion!"

She willed herself to conjure the name to go with the face.

"It's Robby Burke!"

And there it was. She located the essence of him under the twenty-five-year patina.

In July, it's not ideal to hug a humid guy in a tank top whom you haven't seen since high school, but she accepted his one-armed invitation. Sweat contact with a cute man from the town's most famous family is fair game when there isn't any other physical contact in your life.

"What are you doing here?" he asked. "Don't you live in Colorado?"

"California. I'm just here for a week. Helping my dad. You know." *Did he know?* "What about you?" Marion hoped she wouldn't have to go deeper than vague answers about her current life.

"I'm still here. I'm a contractor. Keeps me busy."

He seemed happy. What a shocker, though—she wondered if the rest of the Burkes approved of his not being some kind of lawyer. That profession seemed like a prerequisite for being a Burke: become a lawyer, get elected to some town office, donate money to something worthwhile, get some building or street named after you. Town heroes. That couldn't have been an easy cycle to break.

Marion felt awkward and nervous. At least her tooth was fixed.

"Are you some kind of doctor now?" He smiled. "That'd make sense."

"Oh! No. I'm not. Ha. I . . . No." God, she sounded lame. "I did just go to the dentist. Chipped a tooth." Classy.

"You know, Emily Romero's a dentist. She's good, too. I go to her. Has a brand new office. I used to go to her for math cheat sheets, and now I go to her for teeth cleanings. Crazy. You never know how people are gonna turn out." Robby was oblivious to his sting. He paused, waiting for her to fill the gap in conversation, then gestured toward the street. "Okay, well, I'm off. It's good to see you, Marion." He put his hand on her arm. "Hey, I'm sorry about your mom." So he did know.

"Okay. Bye. Thanks." She was an idiot.

Robby walked toward his truck. "Burke Builders Fine Homes" it said on the side. He looked just as good in that truck as he had in the red '92 Nissan Sentra that had taken him and his friends all over town during high school.

"Hey, Robby!"

"Yeah?"

"I might be here for more than a week."

"Well, they still have half-price jalapeño poppers at Tricorn Pub on Tuesdays," he said, grinning with his arms outstretched. "And I'm still a sucker for the '90s."

CHAPTER III

Marion spread out the documents Emily had given her on the tired twin bed. Her childhood bedroom still smelled the same. The whole house did. Marion wondered how long it could hold on now that her mom was gone. She had prepared herself for her mom's physical absence, but nobody had told her how much the loss would be magnified by all the peripheral blank spots. There were no more overused emojis. No more computer-help questions. No more Mom smells. But Marion was back in town only to help her dad get the house organized now that the funeral was long over and friend visits had subsided.

She inspected the documents: a USGS map of the area, a hand-drawn map of the woods behind the school, a chart about sugar content in drinks, the photo of the woods in the snow, a drawn diagram that matched seasons with senses, and a piece of writing—a magazine clipping. She wondered if Emily had noticed blank spots in her life when Julie disappeared. More than anything, she was mesmerized by the hand-drawn map of the woods behind her old high school—"her woods," it was titled. She recognized it immediately even though she'd never seen it drawn before. The creek, the path, the old stone walls left over from Revolutionary War times. There were some details on there that only someone really familiar with the woods would have noticed. The burn pit was there. It wasn't really a pit, rather a group of rocks that she and Julie and a handful of others, sometimes even Robby, used to sit on to burn their school papers at the end of the year. Watching the flames take away all those papers was mesmerizing. It always smelled good to burn away a year's angst.

This map transported her back to high school. It was so carefully drawn and colored, and from the worn wrinkles it was apparent it had been carried around for quite a long time. The paper was soft from being handled and studied. Each tree was carefully drawn and seemed like it was created just for the person who had made it. The Tang Spot was there too! She smiled. Ms. Turlock, the woman who had worked as the school's main office secretary for as long as Marion could remember, made it a point to bring a few students out to the woods each time the snow was fresh and she was proctoring a study hall. She would always bring her famous jar of Tang. Mixed with snow, it was the ultimate treat. Ms. Turlock thought Tang was a miracle food.

There was a weird, old-style house on the map that she didn't recognize. Near it there was an area marked "berry shrubs," too. Like, bushes? None of this was recognizable to Marion, but it made her nervous. The more she stared at the map, the more her emotions shifted from nostalgia to nervousness. And it made her feel nauseous.

Was this map made as a memento? Who made it? Why? What had happened in these woods—the same woods that had witnessed her teen years? Did it have anything to do with Julie?

The USGS map of the area had the woods area outlined. It was as if someone was trying to understand the surrounding landscape or trying to zoom in from the high-level view to see something more detailed. The USGS map was dated, probably from the 1950s, but not worn out. Route 128, the major highway, was missing, and the roads to the high school today were different. It was an informational map with no hidden agenda.

The magazine clipping was Julie's last piece of writing. Marion almost had it memorized because she'd seen it so many times. The senses map was perplexing. It was done in a hand similar to the hand-drawn map of the woods. It was beautiful. It drew her in. It was like a visualization of Julie's writing. The senses matched up to the last paragraph in the story. Someone had drawn it. And seeing it made her head hurt.

Marion shuffled to the kitchen for some water. There was a stack of framed pictures on the table. Another pile to sort through for her dad.

She lifted the top picture and glanced at the second. It was a painting of snowy woods in the winter. Marion pulled it out. Taped to the back was an unopened card. She tore open the envelope.

Dear Marion,

I am so sorry for your loss. I hope this will help with what you need found.

With love,

Jean Turlock

Marion felt the nerves in the center of her chest light on fire. This painting was so similar to the photo she had from Emily, and this note from Ms. Turlock felt like more than an "I'm sorry your mom's dead" card. It took her only a second to open up the frame, just as Emily had done this morning. Fastened to the back of the canvas was what looked like an incomplete family tree—for Robby Burke's family.

Robby may have invited her only out of sympathy, but now Marion knew she wasn't going to miss tomorrow's jalapeño poppers.

Rufus Burke

Benjamin Burke

George Burke

Chester Burke

Bernadette Shaw !!!

Polly Donati

Edward Burke

Michael Dayton

?

Constance Dayton

Tom Burke

? ?

Lucy Wooten

Judith Parker

Paul Parker

Peter Buchanan

Mary Buchanan

Ernest Parker

Robert Burke

**Burke family tree, given
to Marion by Jean Turlock.**

Craft Deconstruction

Looks matter

At its essence, craft is the visual design of a map. It's what the thing looks like. It's where it's viewed. Craft is how it's made. And with maps, how it's made is what it means.

Methodical destruction

When you're in grade school and want to get a message to a friend across the room, you put that message on a piece of paper, fold it up, and pass it over. That folded note is the vessel that contains your message. With maps, the vessel is craft. Craft is the skin on your data, the house for your frameworks, the front woman for your big ideas. If you're the mapmaker, craft is the filter that everything you want to say must pass through. If you're the viewer, craft is how you orient yourself to understand and react to a map.

We all judge maps based on their craft. It helps convey and expose biases. Intentional craft can make a dense topic float. Sloppy craft can muddy strong points.

Craft is hard to do well. An experienced mapmaker might pull the levers of craft so expertly that every last decision is intentional and has a purpose. A novice might rely on a generic computer program to output a chart in boring computer-blue because they haven't changed the default. Viewers don't know the difference between intention and default.

You can deconstruct maps to examine the role of craft. It's a useful way to make connections between your reactions to a map and the specific levers the mapmaker has pulled to cause those feelings. A straightforward "which, why, how" technique will help you break down any map.

Which emotions?

Look at the map. Ask yourself: What feelings do I get from this map? Excitement? Confusion? Am I shocked? Appalled? Satisfied? Don't worry about why you feel this way. You might have a few emotions. Jot them down.

Why those feelings?

Okay, now worry about *why* you feel this way. Under each emotion, indicate the reason for that emotion. Are you intrigued by the point that the map's trying to make? Are you overwhelmed because none of the labels line up and it's difficult to understand what the map is even about? Are you skeptical because you don't agree with the premise of the map? Are you calm because the colors seem well balanced?

How is that happening?

Now consider the specific decisions or tools the mapmaker used to make these points happen. Some of these decisions relate to data. Others stem from how it was analyzed or what framework is used to show it. Still others are related to biases of the mapmaker or yourself. And of course, many of your reactions to a map are in response to its craft. We'll unpack the specifics of craft next, but try this exercise first. Consider Marion's reaction to the "her woods" map.

HER WOODS MAP DECONSTRUCTION

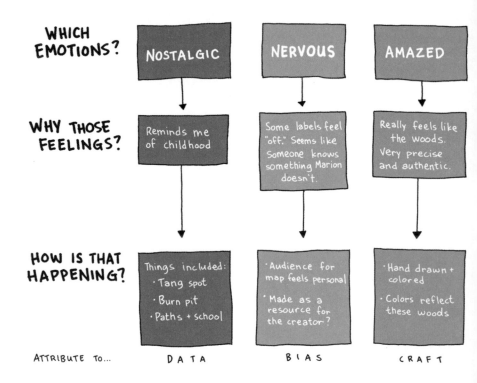

WHICH EMOTIONS?

NOSTALGIC   NERVOUS   AMAZED

WHY THOSE FEELINGS?

Reminds me of childhood

Some labels feel "off." Seems like someone knows something Marion doesn't.

Really feels like the woods. Very precise and authentic.

HOW IS THAT HAPPENING?

Things included:
· Tang spot
· Burn pit
· Paths + school

· Audience for map feels personal
· Made as a resource for the creator?

· Hand drawn + colored
· Colors reflect these woods

ATTRIBUTE TO...   D A T A   B I A S   C R A F T

ROBBY'S FAMILY TREE MAP DECONSTRUCTION

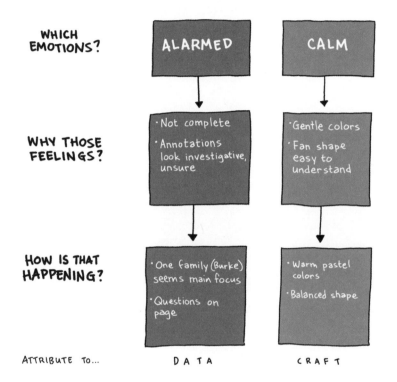

WHICH EMOTIONS?

ALARMED | CALM

WHY THOSE FEELINGS?

- Not complete
- Annotations look investigative, unsure

- Gentle colors
- Fan shape easy to understand

HOW IS THAT HAPPENING?

- One family (Burke) seems main focus
- Questions on page

- Warm pastel colors
- Balanced shape

ATTRIBUTE TO...   DATA   CRAFT

This kind of methodical deconstruction of a map helps you parse the intent and mindset of the creator. It highlights what they did to make you have a given reaction. Remember: craft, bias, and data are always intertwined. They are one. They will always be one. It's usually not possible to attribute a feature of a map solely to one of them, but after deconstructing, you can zoom into craft and examine its raw materials in more detail.

Craft's raw materials

The components of craft are FML CTC: Form, Material, Line, Color, Text, Context. If you like using mnemonic devices to help you remember, this is a good time to create one.

CRAFT

form   color
material text
line   context

Form

Form is another word for shape. Three components of form are especially important when it comes to maps: (1) Canvas shape. What shape is the paper? What size is the screen? (2) Dimension. Is it flat or does it pop out? (3) Graphic shape. What shape is the drawing on the paper?

Canvas shape

A standard size and shape canvas utilizes common elements that exist around us without much modification. If you print your map on letter-size (8.5 by 11 inches) or A4 paper, you are using a standard size canvas. You can pick one up next to a printer anywhere. Ask someone for a sheet of paper, and chances are they'll pull out a sheet of that size. Commonality and familiarity make it standard. What else fits these criteria? Smartphone and computer screens. Of course, there are micro differences depending on brand, but it's pretty standard to view something that spans the screen of a digital device. Nothing about a map in the middle of a newspaper article would give readers pause from its shape. We usually don't notice "standard form canvases" because we're so used to seeing them.

Unconventional canvas shapes can also be physical or digital. A 5-foot by 6-inch poster would force the viewer to either walk along or stand back to see it. They might not be able to take in the whole thing at once. Why would the mapmaker want that type of dimension? Maybe there is a story that unfolds across the map. Maybe the difference between values on the axes are so great that they want to stress the discrepancy. No matter the reason for that uncommon dimensionality, the viewer will notice the deviation from a standard form.

Unconventionality might come from scale, or it might come from shape. What if there were more than four corners? Gasp! What if viewers need to scroll down

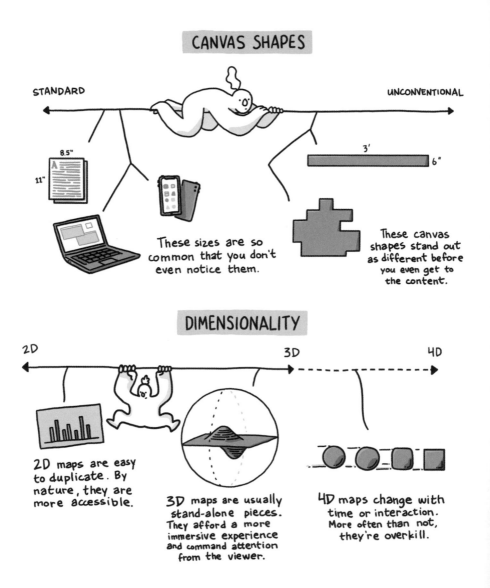

CANVAS SHAPES

STANDARD

UNCONVENTIONAL

8.5"

11"

3'

6"

These sizes are so common that you don't even notice them.

These canvas shapes stand out as different before you even get to the content.

DIMENSIONALITY

2D

3D

4D

2D maps are easy to duplicate. By nature, they are more accessible.

3D maps are usually stand-alone pieces. They afford a more immersive experience and command attention from the viewer.

4D maps change with time or interaction. More often than not, they're overkill.

and keep scrolling to see the bottom of an infographic? They'd certainly notice.

Note: it's not always advantageous to be noticed because of your shape, but intentional use of unconventional canvases is a great way to grab viewers' attention.

Dimension

Is the map flat or bumpy? Does it change with time or interaction? A 2D graphic is easy to duplicate and easier to view than a 3D one. It is accessible by an exponentially larger number of people and is arguably easier to create for most people. Most of us have pens and paper; far fewer have versatility with metal and molds. A 3D map is usually a stand-alone piece. It may command a more focused viewing audience with its dimensionality, and it offers a more

GRAPHIC SHAPES

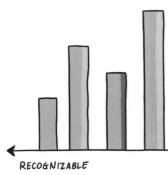

This bar chart is made of... bars.

If the same chart is made out of raised hands, the map conveys an added layer of meaning.

RECOGNIZABLE

UNIQUE

immersive experience to the viewers. We allow ourselves to look at a 3D map longer than we do a 2D version. What about 4D? Things that change with time or interaction? They also command our attention. But be wary of working in 4D. Many 4D infographics are generated digitally and unnecessarily. Things change because the mapmaker found the button to make things change, not because the changing simplifies or accentuates the viewing experience.

Graphic shape

We've talked about canvas shapes; what about the specific shapes of the graphics, marks, and symbols on them? Some might be recognizable and generic, like a bar chart made of . . . wait for it . . . bars. But that same bar chart could be made out of a shape that is unique and important to the data at hand. A bar chart made of lollipops that talks about sugar content in specific foods conveys something about sweets in a subtle way. A bar chart made of raised hands suggests the data might be about people—maybe even people volunteering or being selected.

Material

What is the map made with? Crayons? Construction paper? Faux fur? Pantone 3564 C? Material has meaning.

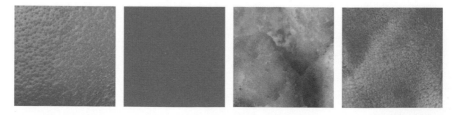

Each of the oranges (below left) is made of a different material. They're all orange, but they each have a different vibe because of the material. Even if your map isn't 3D, if you use a picture or a texture inspired by a physical material, it will give intentional dimension to your content.

Line

You know what a line is, but did you know that the way you make that line matters? Changing the style of your lines can help fine-tune the meaning of your map.

Sketchy and hairy. Unconfident. Humble. Supportive. Confident. Computerized. Overconfident. What is the goal? Are the lines meant to be noticed or just exist in the background?

I'm . . . a car.

I'm practical.

I need you to see me!
I am wild and
possibly dangerous!

I was on sale.

Color

Color merits a textbook unto itself, but when you're examining a map, look at the overlay of color and intent. When deconstructing the use of color in a map, it's useful to think about how and why the creator used color.

Is color used? If not, the map is biased toward being more accessible and reproducible. Not everyone can see the full range of colors, and color prints and copies are harder to make and more expensive. The map might be biasing toward access. It could be clear and to the point without extra colors. It might also need more information or annotation to be understandable.

If it is in color, the map is biased toward being more informative and quickly familiar. The mapmaker gets to play with common color associations to enhance understanding and meaning. Consider what each color is saying in the context of how it's shown.

Text

Words matter. Look at the senses map that Emily gave to Marion. There are words on it. Do they provide enough information? Too much? Where are they? What's their tone? The entire meaning of a map can be twisted using only words.

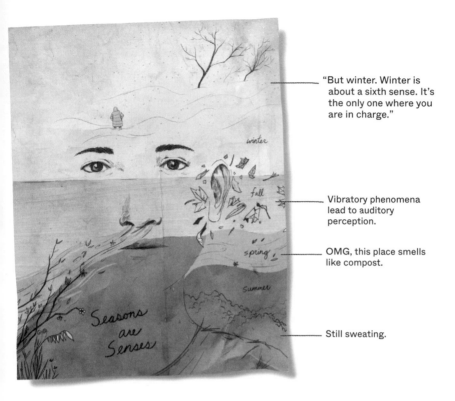

"But winter. Winter is about a sixth sense. It's the only one where you are in charge."

Vibratory phenomena lead to auditory perception.

OMG, this place smells like compost.

Still sweating.

Context

Where was the map made to be viewed? Is it meant to be private and viewed solo? Or is it meant to be seen by many, in groups? Does the creator care where you view it? For some maps, the context is the crux of the map. For others, it doesn't matter.

The quality of craft in a map or infographic is constrained by the abilities of the mapmaker. The tools they know how to use, their sense of style and balance, their ease with words and materials all affect the outcome of the map. The mapmaker's intent might be something more sophisticated than they can accomplish or execute. When deconstructing a map, it can be hard to tell whether a decision was made on purpose or by default. It's usually a bit of both. That's all part of the bias the mapmaker imparts on the map. What you make of it is *your* bias.

Is it something formal to be viewed in a library?

Is it meant to be shared with the world?

Is the map meant to be a secret?

Is it meant to be observed in a group?

CHAPTER IV

Marion had a bit of time before heading to the bar. She parked in the empty lot of Burke High School and started across the blacktop to the woods. At 5:30 on a humid, sticky summer evening, there was plenty of light, not yet raking through the trees. The woods were at least five degrees cooler than the open pavement, and Marion felt less alone and more alone at the same time. Her memories of these woods were all from times when Julie was in her life. Julie loved to sit on the mossy patch near the three trees just beyond view of the first fork in the path. Two oaks and one birch. Most of the moss was the tight, low-to-the-ground bright green type, but some was a bit taller, less of a mat, more wispy. For Marion and Julie, the tight stuff was the right stuff, and there was just enough of it for both of them to squeeze onto, back to back, scrunchie to scrunchie. Moss is always wetter than you want it to be, though, so they'd open a plastic binder, take out the papers, and lay it facedown on the moss. It made a good moisture barrier. Marion always wondered if the pressure of the binder rings was damaging the moss, but it never seemed to.

They could reach out and peel layers from the birch tree's bark, so satisfying to tear off. It's a wonder the tree had survived with the trunk so naked in spots. Sitting on the mossy patch, the girls weren't totally out of sight, but they were pretty well hidden and could always see people approaching before they were noticed.

Marion walked up to the fork, left the trail, and found where the mossy patch should have been. Dead leaves. Mushrooms. It was mossless. She leaned her back against the birch tree and stared into the warm forest. This spot wasn't marked on the map.

Her eyes welled with tears. She let them overflow through closed lids for a minute.

What kind of friend abandons her best friend? What kind of friend lets her best friend vanish? What happened to Julie? Marion knew she had to figure it out.

She wiped her face and took a breath. Then she followed the map. She sought out each marked spot and took it in, hoping for a clue.

The burn pit, where they had their yearly burn-outs, was overgrown. The rocks that had ringed it were nearby, but no longer in a circle. Now that everything happened on a computer, maybe its time had passed. The old low stone walls were the same. They didn't register twenty-five years of age, given they'd already seen close to three hundred years. Modern teenage love, WWII lookout patrols, militias battling the British to kickstart a country. What else had these walls witnessed?

Marion's feet sank a couple of inches into the decomposing leaves that clustered near the walls. Dirt was finding its way up the sides of her shoes.

As she moved along the map's route, she could see that the Tang Spot was still there! It looked now like a place where someone still came to smoke cigarettes. They were strewn everywhere. There was an old glass jar of Tang in the middle of the circle and a volcano of cigarette butts. The label was gone, but the glass had the letters in relief. Marion needed to find Ms. Turlock and see why she'd given her the family tree. Did Ms. Turlock even know the Tang Spot was still there?

Marion then approached the place where the map was marked "Last Stand." There was no path here. There was lots of brush with poison ivy. It was hard to walk on the uneven ground. Marion didn't linger.

She started toward the mystery house, and the berry shrubs that were labeled on the map. She didn't remember berries in these woods, but in high school she'd focused on not feeling stupid, not on foraging. There was definitely never a house there.

Still no house. No berries. She studied the map and slowly spun in a circle. There was a clearing, and it seemed possible that a small structure could have been there, but there wasn't even a remnant today.

Marion walked through the tall grass to the middle of the small clearing. *Gotta do a tick check later,* she thought to herself. There was a mound of rocks, fortyish round ones, the size of large hamburger buns. Marion stared down. Tall grass grew between the stones. The stones seemed comfortable in their cuddle, but a patch of grass had been torn out by hand in front of the pile to make some space. And a single lily, its stem cut cleanly, had been laid in front of the stone pile. The lily was fresh and firm, a recent gift in honor. This was a grave.

The hair on her neck rose, and she whipped around, looking for another person. Who had put that flower here? She looked at the map. Berry shrubs. Who talks that way? The language felt slightly off. And this was not a place for berries. It was more like a burial site.

The nervousness she'd felt when she first looked at the map was back. Was she standing on Julie's grave?

CHAPTER V

"Emily, have you seen Julie since she disappeared?"

"What? No, of course not."

"Sorry. I had to ask." There was a long pause, and they were both grateful for the phone barrier. Marion didn't know how to talk about the grave—assuming it was a grave. She wondered if Emily knew about it. It seemed like this type of thing would have been found when they searched for her. Unless maybe it was better hidden then. Or maybe it wasn't a grave.

"I'm sorry, Marion. I gotta apologize. It's been so long. I never expected to see you again, and then there you were, and I wasn't thinking, and all I've ever wanted is for her to come back or at least to know . . . and then you came to the office . . . and then, I knew there was something behind the picture, but I never knew what, and I thought maybe you would help, but . . . I'm sorry, I know it's not fair of me. It's all my fault anyway. I made this happen . . . it shouldn't be your pr—"

"Emily, stop. What's going on? You made what happen?"

"I don't know. The whole mess. Sorry."

"Emily, what are you talking about?"

"I shouldn't have given you that stuff yesterday. I'm sorry. I'll swing by later and grab it from you. I'll deal with it."

"Emily, what? I said I'd help." *Did I say that?* "What do you mean, you made this happen?"

There was a pause.

"Emily?"

Emily inhaled. "That January."

"That January *what?*" Marion wasn't going to let Emily back-pedal out of this.

"I made Julie disappear. Okay? Are you satisfied?"

Marion was dumbstruck.

Emily kept going. "I must have. There's just no way. It was a messed-up time. I was a wreck. She wasn't exactly excited about college, though."

"What did you do, Emily?" Marion was wary. Emily seemed like a mostly normal adult now, but Marion couldn't forget the hyper-cool teenage snark that used to lace her language.

"Nothing! I don't know. I didn't even think to do anything else." Her voice faltered; she was barely able to get the words out: "I p-probably killed her."

"What do you mean?"

"Julie was helping me. She was covering for me. Again. She knew it was me. Then she was gone. She'd still be here if I hadn't been such a screw-up."

"What? Covering for you?"

"That night at school. Over winter break. Come on. You know. Don't make me say it all."

"Emily, I don't know what you mean." Marion kept her voice level.

"I stole the history tests and ran right by you. There was no other way out. I needed the money and a good grade, and I knew that room was always open. I just didn't think you guys would be there, too."

Marion lifted her head from the phone in shock.

"What? That was you?! Why didn't you say something? Did Julie know? Was Julie in on it?" Marion was taken completely by surprise, maybe even angry—all these years later—at being left out. Of course Julie wouldn't have wanted to tell on Emily. She was always covering for her. Still, it was hard to learn that Julie hadn't confided in her. It's not like Marion would have betrayed that trust—at least, she didn't think she would've.

"No, Julie wasn't part of it. She'd never do something like that. You know that."

"Why would you do that? I don't get it."

"You wouldn't. Look—I had planned to be in and out. You weren't there when I arrived, but it took me a few minutes to find the tests and an envelope. As I was about to leave, I saw you. I knew right away it was the two of you."

"But you didn't say anything."

"Come on. I was a stupid high school kid. I tried to run at you to scare you. I thought it would be funny. But you didn't move, and I just kept going. I knew I was caught, though. Julie knew."

"I didn't know it was you," said Marion. "I was so scared that I'd be in trouble for being in there."

"Yeah, well, Julie stared me down as I ran by."

Marion sank deeper into Julie's betrayal.

"She never told me." Now Marion was annoyed with herself. *Come on! Why are you making this about you?*

"Sorry. I didn't know," said Emily. "She told you everything. I figured she told you about this, too. If it helps, when she came home that night she tore my head off for an hour. I was cramming on the tests, making some notes. I knew she was gonna be pissed, but this was beyond that. She just let me have it. On and on. She was right, too. I was a mess. Making nothing of myself. Going to get expelled for doing something stupid. She said she was done covering for me. I kinda pretended like I didn't care, but I knew she was serious. She just seemed different."

"Wait—Emily, I'm coming over. We should go through everything together."

"I'm still at work. I have two more patients."

Marion still couldn't believe that Rebel Emily had patients.

"I'll come later, then. I was going to meet up with Robby Burke at the pub anyway."

Emily seemed to be waiting, letting Marion fill the pause.

"He invited me," Marion fumbled. She had a need to fill the space in a conversation. "But not like a date."

Emily didn't say anything. Then she exhaled, and now her voice was strong, emphatic: "Be careful, Marion." It wasn't clear what she was warning her about.

CHAPTER VI

Marion stared at the bartender's headpiece. It was hard to believe that tricorn hats were ever fashionable. Why would anyone take a hat with a wide, round brim and fold up the edges to make a triangle-type shape? Below the hat brim, his hair was greasy. What was the point of the folded-up brim? Wouldn't rain collect in the hat gutters and pour out directly in front of the wearer's nose? A personal water fountain? His hat probably smelled like 1775.

Robby's shape snagged her peripheral vision. He was outside of Tricorn Pub, finishing a phone call. His brow was furrowed. He looked older than he was, like he'd been through a lot. His body seemed well-suited to be a contractor, though. She wondered how his family treated him since he'd deviated from the traditional Burke path.

After a minute, he hung up and walked into the pub alone.

"Marion? You came." He seemed more surprised than excited to see her. He smelled like sawdust.

"Robby. You just cut some wood?" *Great opening line.*

"Kinda the essence of the job." He seemed more deflated than he'd been the other day.

"I ordered us jalapeño poppers!" she tried to counter with enthusiasm.

"Ah. Right." Robby nodded at the bartender. "Jonas." A beer appeared in front of him. "Soooo . . . what's up, Marion?"

"Oh—I guess . . . I'll have one, too." She got the bartender's attention and pointed at Robby's beer. "What's up? I, uh, nothing. Just finding myself in town for a bit and you said I should come . . . It's been a crazy week." *Bring it back, Marion.*

"You and me both." He took a long sip.

Marion was instantly gutted. He cocked his head to the left to look at her, but his body made it clear that if he was on a date with anyone, it was with the beer. Even so, she decided to just go for it.

"Do you remember Ms. Turlock from high school?"

"Of course. Tang Spot. She's nuts. Still works at the school. Getting old, losing her marbles. Why?" Another looong sip.

"Actually, what if I told you she was a bit obsessed with you?"

Robby laughed knowingly and swirled the glass.

"Like she's been trying to map your family tree."

"My family tree?" He didn't look as amused as he was trying to sound. His eyebrows were too high. "Everyone in this town knows my family tree. Every member of my family is a friggin' open book. You don't have to be obsessed with me to know my family tree. As far as I'm concerned, she can have my family tree, but she needs to leave me the frick alone."

He finished his beer and put a ten on the counter. He'd hardly looked at Marion during their short meeting, and he was leaving before the jalapeño poppers.

"But the jalapeño poppers." *Ultimate idiot.*

He stood, put a patronizing hand on her arm, and kissed the top of her head. Sweat and sawdust. "You enjoy mine. So good to catch up, Marion. Don't be worrying about Tang Spot and her conspiracy theories now. I know you and your friends used to be all buddy-buddy with her back in the day, but she's a nutjob now."

She noticed his armpit hair poking out from his tank top. But it didn't matter what he said or how he looked—she found him intoxicating. *What the hell is wrong with me?*

CHAPTER VII

Emily opened the door before Marion made it up the walk. She waved her in.

As soon as she stepped inside, it seemed to Marion that the house felt off. Emily was always so cool. Her home should have been modern. Sparse. At least clean. Instead, it was like a cluttered, artsy souvenir store. Tiny elephant figurines. Corn cob dolls. Origami ducks. Dream catchers. Nesting dolls. Artwork and tapestries. Crystals and incense.

Emily seemed to know what Marion was thinking. "I kept all the stuff from Julie's room." She gestured toward a different part of the house. "I re-created how she had it set up. You know how she loved all her little things. Her collections and trinkets. Always saving every paper and tiny sketch and love note. I couldn't get rid of it. What if she came back? Then I just began . . . I dunno . . . expanding it." She gestured at the whole room, then touched a tiny wind chime. "I actually take trips to places Julie talked about. I try to pursue her interests. If I do things she would have liked, I still feel her around me. I know it's—"

"You don't have to explain. I get it." Marion didn't know this side of Emily. But that wasn't what she had come here for. "Tell me more about that night."

Emily clicked back into herself. "That was it, mostly. I took the tests. I was stupid. I had fifty bucks coming in for it. Ten people were going to chip in to be able to see all those old test questions. That's a lot when you're sixteen. But obviously I never got it." She raised her eyebrows at Marion.

"Huh?"

"Julie took back all the tests. That same night. After we'd had it out for a while."

"And then what?"

"Then nothing. She was in and out those next few days, and then she was just out. Forever. She was so pissed at me. It changed something." Emily was staring into space.

"Did you do something to her?" Marion barely squeaked out the question.

"WHAT?! Of course not. Seriously, Marion." Emily waited a second. "It was just like—after that night she turned into a shell of herself. And I never got a chance to apologize."

Marion put her hand on Emily's shoulder. The touch seemed to zap Emily back to the present. She stood up quickly. "I gotta get to bed, Marion. I really do appreciate your help." She stuck her hand out with dentist formality.

Marion scrunched up her face in surprise. "Wait. Can I show you one thing first?" Marion pulled out the Burke family tree map. "I found this today."

Emily was walking toward the door, not looking at her.

Marion continued, "It's Robby Burke's family tree."

"Ha. Did he give you that on your date?"

"It wasn't a date. No. He was weird about it, too."

Emily came back. "Let me see it." She pulled the map from Marion's hands, studied it, then looked back up at Marion. "Bernadette Shaw? Where'd you get this, Marion?" This had woken her up.

"I found it b—"

"I know that name. The poem was about her. From the 1799 letter."

"What?"

"Sort of a letter. From 1799. It had a letter and a poem on it. That old angled cursive that was so hard to read."

"A letter from 1799? What are you talking about?"

"It was hidden in between all the tests. Julie returned it with everything else, but I saw it. It didn't mean much to me. I figured it was part of the test because it was from Rufus Burke—you know, our big Revolutionary War hero? Some sort of historical document. They were history tests."

"Did Julie see it? What did she say about it?"

"I don't know. Maybe. Probably. Why?" Emily was talking fast. "Do you think it's important? Did you show this to Robby?"

"No—I mentioned it, but I didn't show him."

"Don't show him. He'll just get upset. He's been all over the place lately. Hey, don't tell him about any of this, okay? He's a sweetie, but his family is tough. Obsessed with 'giving back' to the town and showing the rest of us how generous they are. So they donate scholarship money every year—big deal. Give someone else a shot. You should see this poster his dad has begun to put up for the election. He's running for school committee. Idiotic. There're fliers with it, too. Look."

She pulled out a paper from her purse and put it in Marion's hands. Vote Tom Burke!

"See this graph. It makes it seem like all that money they give to the school has something to do with lowering the dropout rate. Those two things aren't even related! Just because they have family money. Whatever. If they all want to keep kidding each other, that's fine. It's so obviously messed up. Can you believe they still bug Robby about being a contractor? It's all he ever wanted to do. But whatever. Everyone's got issues, I guess." She paused. "He's been real nice to me ever since Julie left. Kinda took care of me for a while."

Emily was still looking down at the family tree. When she finally looked up, the tears in her eyes were mirrored in Marion's. But it wasn't clear if they were crying about the same things.

The Tom Burke election poster seen all around town.

CHAPTER VIII

The next morning, Marion returned to the pile of stones in the clearing. The lily was wilted now.

"What's so great about Robby Burke anyway?" Marion muttered to herself. She was always more objective, less emotional, in the morning.

She looked down at Julie's grave. "Does he know who did this to you?" She had to tell someone about finding the grave, but she just wanted one more moment alone with her best friend. Twenty-five lost years. "Did you get in his way? His family's way?"

Sweat was pooling in her creases. Her body never harmonized with heat and humidity.

Julie had always been the easiest person for her to talk to. Marion thought back to the last time she'd seen her. The argument over whether to report the strange runner at school was so intense. It wasn't like them to fight. Julie had insisted on letting it go. Keeping quiet. Marion always felt like there was something she didn't know. "What aren't you telling me? We might be the only witnesses to a crime!" And Julie had shouted back, "Enough! I'm done!" and stormed home.

She thought about Julie's writing and the beautiful "senses" map that seemed to match it. It was as though someone was honoring her. She thought of the sugar chart with maple syrup and Tang. So odd. She thought of the basket of jalapeño poppers she'd eaten by herself last night. She was so lame but those poppers were so delicious. She started to think about Robby and then stopped herself with a mental image of his armpits. Julie would have laughed.

"I get it now," she said to the pile of stones. "I'm sorry, Julie. Now I know you were protecting Emily. But I don't know why anyone would do this to you. Does she?"

Then a chirpy voice startled her from behind. "Julie? Sorry, Marion, but you're talking to the wrong dead person!"

Marion whipped around and looked up. She saw a smaller, softer shape, a wrinkled face, and a gentle smile. "Ms. Turlock?"

Bias Deconstruction
Mind the message

There's an ambiguous force at play in every map—it can feel like an unease in the center of the chest. What's included and what isn't? How is it depicted? Taken in? Is it useful? Enlightening? Dangerous or empowering? This force is bias. Your bias is your preference. It's your intuition. It's shaped by your perspective. It's born from your culture, your lived experiences, and your current context. Your bias is the lens through which you view the world. Sometimes that lens is sharp. Other times it's blurry. But you and me—odds are we don't wear the same prescription.

As a viewer of a map, you need to be aware of your own biases, as well as those of the mapmaker. With each map you examine, consider the intent of its creator. What is the point of the map? Does it have a baked-in agenda? Did they aim to create a map that puts a specific topic in focus for a certain type of person? Are they hoping to get you lost in a house of mirrors? To steer your attention in a certain direction? Have they forgotten that they even wear lenses?

Bias is an undercurrent to both craft and data. The latter two are the ways in which bias manifests in a map. Sometimes a mapmaker has a clear bias, a point they want to make, something they choose to prioritize. This is their agenda. That agenda comes to life through their craft and data decisions.

Bias's raw materials

Bias is tricky. It's an interconnected web, and the elements aren't sequential. When you deconstruct a map for bias, pay attention to these three elements: the viewer's reaction, the creator's intent, and the bias's "cloud"—the qualities that make up bias itself.

BIAS
cloud
reaction
intention

Viewer's reaction

What's the impact of the map on the viewer? What is the viewer's reaction to the map? What emotions does it evoke? Why?

Creator's intent

Does the map have an agenda? A point it is trying to make? A specific context or target audience?

Bias cloud

What are the features or qualities of the bias? Is it explicit or implicit? Harmful or harmless? Hidden or obvious?

Bias in the viewer's reaction

If you are the viewer, what's your relationship to the topic of the map? What parts of your worldview affect your interpretation of the map?

We're all experts on ourselves, and it's both hardest and easiest to start there. It's hard to see beyond our own experiences. It's easy to talk about our own preferences. In the illustration at right, do you prefer the bright red or light pink? Why?

I like the bright red. It feels like it has guts and likes to go out and have fun. The light pink seems too gentle. It's not a color I want to wear. It won't look good on me. It feels too cutesy and stereotypically girly. These are my preferences, my biases. They are based on my lived experiences. I've never identified with light pink as a "girl" color. I never liked dolls or a lot of the toys that were dressed in light pink. It doesn't represent me, but a lot of society says

that it should, so my reaction is to challenge it. I have experienced gender bias, and I always notice it and want to challenge it to the tiniest detail. This means light pink to me. The bright red feels more like how I want to be—bold and exciting. It's aspirational. It doesn't feel like a gendered color. My experiences, my culture, and my context all shape my bias and my preference for the bright red. Your reaction is likely just as nuanced in its own way.

There's no map here. These are just colors. Put these colors on a map, and they bring the baked-in biases with them. Color adds a layer of meaning, but that meaning will vary from person to person.

YOUR RELATIONSHIP. YOUR REACTION.

If this is you, and this is the topic of the map, what is your gut reaction to the map?

Are you excited, energized by what it's showing?

Does it feel welcoming? Do you want to explore it?

Do you see it for what it is and want to organize it your way?

Do you want to flush it?

Is it daunting? Overwhelming? Scary?

Articulate your bias

When deconstructing a map for bias, take in the content, then make sense of your gut reaction. At first, this reaction might be blobby and amorphous.

Let yourself react, then force yourself to articulate where that reaction originates. Is the map shocking because it's showing you something you never expected? Are you skeptical because you are an expert in the field it's depicting, and you have insider knowledge? Do you have personal experience with one of the themes in the map that might cause you to react in one way or another? Your reaction is valid. But be aware that the specifics and limitations of your own lived experience will color your interpretations.

Bias in the creator's intent

Who is the mapmaker? What is the agenda of their map? Is there an insight, something the mapmaker discovered that they are trying to show? A hook? Are the mapmaker's biases well known to the world? Do you have a hunch? Can you find them out? In other words, if you know the person who created the map, or an organization they are part of, you might be able to figure out their values and their biases.

EVERY MAP HAS AN AGENDA

AMOUNT OF AGENDA (vertical axis)

INVITE
HERE'S AN IDEA. LOOK INSIDE AND SEE WHAT YOU MAKE OF IT.

TELL
THIS IS THE RIGHT STUFF. I DON'T CARE WHAT YOU DO WITH IT.

REVEAL
TADA! I BET YOU NEVER EXPECTED THAT?

MANIPULATE
"THESE AREN'T THE DROIDS YOU'RE LOOKING FOR."

MAPMAKER'S INTENT (horizontal axis)

Every map has an agenda

The intent behind a map can vary.

Some maps are made to invite a viewer to explore a topic, to plant a seed of an idea. Others are made to tell the viewer about a topic with a degree of confidence, but the viewer can draw their own conclusions. Others are made to reveal an idea that might be otherwise unknown. And of course, some maps are made with a goal of manipulation.

What are the agendas of some of the maps that Marion uncovered?

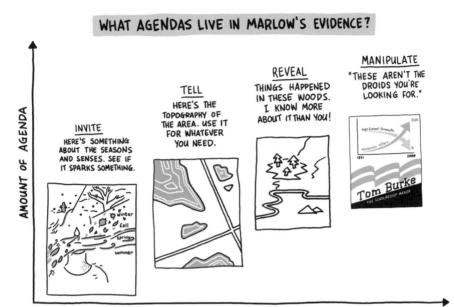

AMOUNT OF AGENDA

INVITE
HERE'S SOMETHING
ABOUT THE SEASONS
AND SENSES. SEE IF
IT SPARKS SOMETHING.

winter
fall
spring
summer

TELL
HERE'S THE
TOPOGRAPHY OF
THE AREA. USE IT
FOR WHATEVER
YOU NEED.

REVEAL
THINGS HAPPENED
IN THESE WOODS.
I KNOW MORE
ABOUT IT THAN YOU!

MANIPULATE
"THESE AREN'T THE
DROIDS YOU'RE
LOOKING FOR."

High School Dropouts
Scholarship offers
1971   2000

Tom Burke
THE SCHOLARSHIP MAKER

MAPMAKER'S INTENT

The senses map feels like an invitation. At this point in the story, it is unclear who made it or why. We know it relates to some prose. It doesn't feel like it's trying to spur Marion to any action, one way or the other, but if it ends up being something sinister, this map could end up having more agenda than it seems to right now. The USGS map tells about the topography of the landscape. It was made to show what's there, but the viewer gets to choose how to use the information. The map of the woods feels like a "reveal." There are clues on it, like "Last Stand," that seem to indicate the creator wants the viewer to see something new. However, this could be wrong. We don't know the creator. Marion was made nervous by that map, and the creator might indeed have a sinister intent. Don't forget that the context for these maps is a missing person case. They are clues. It helps to try to place them, but it's likely you'll make an error, because a lot of information is unknown.

What about the graph on the Tom Burke campaign poster? (See page 53.) Use it to test your ability to read bias. Deconstruct it, and then examine the components of bias at play.

This one is clearly meant to manipulate. The phrasing of the title is meant to indicate that if you vote for Tom Burke for school committee (and he prevails), more scholarships will be awarded and fewer people will drop out of high school. Green is the color of money. Red, in this context, appears to indicate something disturbing—dropouts. That the poster is displayed in public places shows that the intent is for lots of people to see it quickly. These are all details of craft that show the bias of the creator.

However, there are decisions about data in here that are also heavily influenced by bias. First, there is no y-axis, the vertical axis. Actually, this plot should have two vertical axes. One should show dollar values. The other should show number of dropouts. Without the axes, the viewer conflates the two, and it seems like the number of high school dropouts started near 750,000 and is now down to four. Second, the two things that are being

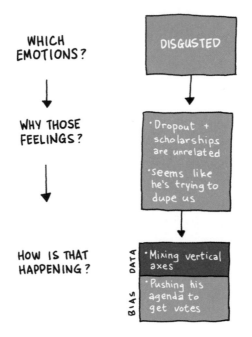

depicted—scholarship dollars and high school dropouts—
are measured in totally different values, but they are
presented as if they are related. Tom Burke wants the
voters to think that increasing scholarships causes fewer
students to drop out. Correlation and causation aside,
these are likely not steady, linear changes, yet the map
depicts them as such over an almost 150-year period.

Mind the message

Bias clouds

Bias can be anywhere on the continuum from harmless to dangerous. Ask three questions to pinpoint which features are at play:

Is the creator aware of the bias?

Is it announced on the map?

Does it hurt people?

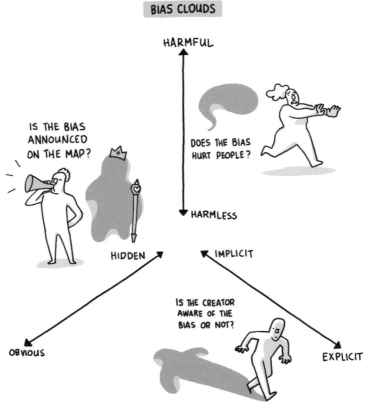

The "Vote Tom Burke" poster is an election campaign piece. Its bias cloud looks something like this:

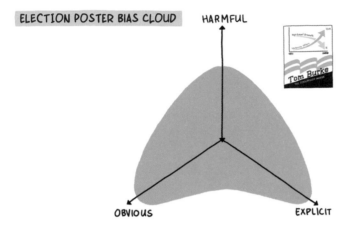

The bias cloud of the USGS topographic map looks something like this:

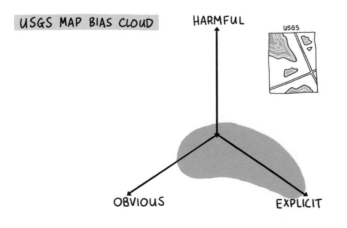

Tom Burke has a strong desire to make a point. He wants to be elected. It's his purpose for building the map. It's his explicit bias. Explicit biases may or may not be shown in a bold, obvious way, though. They could be subtle.

Explicit biases aren't necessarily bad things, either. The USGS topographic map has an explicit bias, too. It's prioritizing topography. The agency is not trying to manipulate anyone to vote for it, but its agenda is clear.

An implicit bias by the mapmaker is a specific belief that gets assimilated into both the data and the craft. This is muscle memory and automatic—do something enough, and it's second nature.

Always making female things pink and male things blue shows an implicit bias, both for gender norms and colors, but also for two—and only two—genders. Pink is a reinforcing signal that there is a specific way for women to express themselves. For many people, this would be harmless. But we should be wary, because it's not. For people who are gender nonconforming, it's another reminder of being outsiders. Taken as a one-off, it might not hurt too much. Taken in aggregate from all of society, it's a full body of pain.

As always, whether or not a bias is harmful has a lot to do with the full context of how it plays out. There is a big difference between saying "I like the color green" and "I hire only green people." Racism, sexism, classism, and ableism are all part of the many existing systems of oppression. In the context of a book about maps, it's important to know that these institutionalized biases affect different people in different ways.

The cultural context and lived experiences of the creator and viewer matter. Creators should take seriously what they make because of the impact on others and the norms created or reinforced, whether intentionally or not.

Our biases are ever-present. They're expressed in how we craft our maps, and they're part of our decision making as we collect and use the data that powers them.

CHAPTER IX

Marion hugged Ms. Turlock, ignoring the fact that her own sweaty body presented an adhesive surface and might not ever peel away from the old front office secretary. Robby might think the lady is nuts, but Ms. Turlock was one of Marion's favorite people from high school. She and Julie would always chat with her on their way out, always want to be taken out to the Tang Spot. Ms. Turlock was a comfort. Marion inhaled the Crabtree & Evelyn Summer Hill scent that Ms. Turlock used to cover up the smell of cigarettes. How did she still have that scent? Marion's mom used to love those sachets. Do people use sachets anymore? When the rest of the school was a cloud of citrusy Gap Dream perfume—spritzed from the lipstick-shaped dispenser—walking into the front office always came with a gust of flowery Summer Hill.

"It's so good to see you, Ms. Turlock."

"Call me Jean, darling. Oh Marion, you're just the same. I was sorry to hear about your mother." Ms. Turlock looked her up and down. Marion tried to smile.

They both turned and looked down at the pile of stones. Marion asked, "Whose grave is this, then?"

"Say hello to Bernadette Shaw."

"Bernadette Shaw? She was on the family tree you gave me."

"Ahhh." Ms. Turlock was noticeably pleased.

"I'm still not sure why you gave it to me, though." Marion thought she'd asked a question, but it wasn't answered.

Ms. Turlock continued, "Bernadette Shaw turned the tide during the American Revolution." Her face had gone stern, and she jabbed her index finger down toward the grave with each *she*: "*She* was elected captain of the minutemen in the local militia at a time when women didn't do that sort of thing. *She* trained a group of more than fifty men in the art of surprise warfare! *She* led the battle that sent the British retreating to Boston."

Ms. Turlock was almost shouting, ecstatically: "*Her* feats put this town on the map!" Then she took a breath and proceeded more calmly: "*She* made this country possible."

"Until the family tree, I'd never heard of her." Marion's admission made Ms. Turlock's face fall.

"You've heard of Rufus Burke, though. The namesake for our high school. Burke everything, right? Bastards."

Marion nodded. *Bastards?*

"Rufus was a private in Bernadette's militia. He was wounded, and she stood over him, firing her musket in protection until the British retreated."

Marion stared as Ms. Turlock pretended to load ammunition into the muzzle of a musket, jam it down with a ramrod, then hoist it to her shoulder to fire. "Rufus was fine with having his life saved, but it was too much that it had been done by a woman. He stabbed her with his bayonet and stood over her body until other privates found them." Ms. Turlock clutched her stomach as if she'd taken the hit. "She was so badly injured, she couldn't speak." She paused, then added eagerly, "But I can! And you can. We can do it together!"

"Wait—do what together?"

"Keep up, Marion! I'm sick of waiting." It wasn't clear what she'd been waiting for, but she continued, "Rufus claimed that it was *he* who had protected Bernadette, firing shots, taking on an injury himself. He kept up that story until right before his death."

Marion wasn't quite sure what role she was playing in this reenactment. Then Ms. Turlock clarified, "You think Rufus Burke was the man who saved this town? You think he was a hero? You think all the Burkes are heroes, with their fancy jobs and generous donations? You're just like all of them!"

"Ms. Turlock, are you okay?"

She settled back into her usual gentle demeanor and met Marion's eyes. "With glory came power, and with power came money, and it set the Burke family on a course that persists today."

"So you're saying that Rufus Burke wasn't a hero? He killed this woman, Bernadette Shaw?" Marion pointed at the grave. "And the Burkes are living a lie? All of them? How do you know all this?"

Ms. Turlock had her hands on her hips. "The Burkes," she gestured toward the school, "are living one of *the* biggest cover-ups in the history of this country."

Then she abruptly turned her back on Marion and began walking away.

"Ms. Turlock? Wait." Marion was confused.

Ms. Turlock called back, a disgusted look on her face, "Like maple syrup, that family. Seems delicious, but it's really bad for you." With that, she kept walking. Her back to Marion, she raised a hand and waved her off.

Maybe Robby was a little bit right, and she isn't as mentally in tune as she used to be. But what is it with the Burkes?

CHAPTER X

Marion wriggled through Burke High School's cracked F-Block window and dropped into the room in much the same way she often entered a swimming pool, with an unintended belly flop. But it was the only possible landing after getting in through the sole breach in the school fortress. Even the smokers' door was locked.

She crouched for a minute, listening for any sign that she'd been noticed. No alarms.

She stood up. Her cheap sneaker rubber soles squeaked so loudly on the linoleum that they might as well have been homing beacons for anyone within a mile radius. Shoes off. In sock feet, Marion made her way to the school office. She half expected to find Ms. Turlock at her desk even though it was Saturday, but the room was empty. Where to begin? Open some drawers. Folders with dates—class rosters. Marion Marlow, class of 1995. Julie Romero, class of 1995. Nothing she didn't know. There had to be something useful about the Burkes in here somewhere. The Burkes from her parents' generation had often been around here—hanging with the principal in the office, doing who knows what.

Marion sat down in Ms. Turlock's chair and looked up at the wall. The huge brass plaque honoring the Burke family scholarship winners had twice the footprint as she remembered. *Imagine staring at that all day*, she thought. *It's no surprise Ms. Turlock's a bit obsessed.*

Burke Family Scholars: "As you are now, so once was I. As I am now, so you must be."—Rufus Burke

Underneath the quote were etched at least 150 names stretching back to the 1860s. *They've seeped into everything.* Emily Romero,

1997. So Emily was a winner. She must have really turned her act around during the last year of high school. There were more winners after 1997. Marion thought about Tom Burke's campaign flier—seven hundred fifty thousand dollars in scholarships. Does it count as a good deed if you can't stop bragging about it? Marion took a few photos of the wall of names. Maybe the scholarships were a clue.

Marion turned and opened the door to the principal's office. Unfinished wood from half-constructed bookshelves made the place smell like pine. The drop cloth protecting the carpeting crinkled underfoot as she made her way to the principal's computer.

Of course, she needed a password. You can't just will yourself to become a hacker.

Marion went upstairs to the school library. It was open. It's interesting how libraries and bookstores, both repositories for the same things, have different aromas. You'd know either one blindfolded. Bookstores are fit and freshly showered twenty-somethings. Libraries are their slightly out-of-shape older friends who get winded walking up a flight of stairs. No wonder she felt at home here.

She pulled out a chair and sat at a computer. This, she could dominate. "Burke Family Scholarship"—a few hits from the local paper about recent winners. "Burke Family Scholarship Emily Romero"—no results. No online records prior to 2006. But microfilm was still a thing, and Marion was back in her element.

She went year by year in reverse. For all of the recent years it was easy to find both the winners and the financial amounts of their scholarships. The town's weekly paper, ever the champion of the Burkes, never failed to congratulate the family and remind the reward recipients of their great honor. It always appeared in the graduation issue, usually the second or third week of June. She found records going back to 1871, when the paper began publishing.

Year. Scholarship Winner Name. Financial Award. 1997. Emily Romero. $40,000. Easily the highest value she'd seen in her search. There were no winners in 1996.

Marion was so confused that she didn't hear the truck pull up.

CHAPTER XI

"Hello?" Robby's voice rang in the stairwell as he clumped up the stairs.

Marion hit the floor. She crawled behind the stacks and froze. How did he know she was here?

He continued, "Ms. Turlock? Ms. Turlock? I know you're here."

Did he know it was her and not Ms. Turlock? Marion did her best to become one with the carpet.

"Ms. Turlock, look. I know what you think, but I'm not like them. I didn't start all this." He walked over to the computer she had open. Shit.

"I know you know about the money. They never told me. It's all guilt money. But it goes to good causes. I was never good enough for them. I swear. When I started the bookcases and you told me, that was the first I heard about it. I want to make it right."

Marion breathed silently. She heard not a sound. He was still there.

"Look, Ms. Turlock. It's messed up. I get that. The family knows you know. You gotta take it down a notch. Stop the sneaking. I can help you. You could retire. Paint. Doodle your days away."

She waited.

"Fine. Suit yourself. But no more funny business with Marion. I know you're dropping hints. I don't want to have to mop up that mess, too."

Data Deconstruction
The D word

Data! Finally, the meat of the map. Vegetarians welcome.

There's often a tendency to rush into THE DATA. It's important, yes. Data is your raw material. It's the information that is sought, molded, stretched, and reconstituted into what becomes the map. Without data, there is nothing to make a map about. But data is Jell-O. It's quite easy to give it any shape or flavor and it'll look good on the plate. Ta-da! It might even be delicious. At the risk of pushing that metaphor too far, a great-tasting, intricate-looking Jell-O mold isn't necessarily good for you. The same holds true for maps and infographics. Enjoy the data, but don't be fooled. When deconstructing a map through the lens of data, remember that it is inextricable from bias and craft.

"What does the data say?"

Trick question. Don't ask the data! It can't talk. People are the talkers. Instead, ask "What does the creator of this map want this data to mean?" Or "What does the creator of this map think this data can show us?" This slight reframing can help keep bias and craft top of mind. Even the simplest data set will be interpreted differently by two different creators.

Types of data

There are some data basics when it comes to maps. Data can be quantitative, qualitative, or mixed.

Quantitative data is a pile of numbers. Qualitative data is a pile of observations. Mixed data is some of both. All of these require a human to make meaning out of them. Some people think that quantitative data is better. But "better" isn't the right word. With today's computers, quantitative data is easier to work with at scale. It's easier and faster to process. But qualitative data is a treasure trove of nuance and possibility.

Consider a simple sentence: "I'd love to do that." Now think of all the different ways you might put emphasis on the different words in that sentence and alter its meaning entirely. The way you say the words matters. Are you genuine? Sarcastic? Do you point at something unexpected while emphasizing *that* in order to convey a surprise? Are you speaking to someone who is from your culture, someone who understands the tiny twitch in your face as you emphasize *love*? It's hard for us, human to human, to make sense of each other, but this is what qualitative data is—that pile of observations. It's messy, hard for people to process, and even harder for machines to process—they don't have your sense of humor. So qualitative data is trickier to work with, but potentially richer in what might be mined out of it. Some of the most interesting data sets are mixed—number values combined with motivations. No matter the type of data, it needs a human to make meaning out of it.

DATA BOUNDARIES ARE NEVER CLEAR-CUT

You can collect data from anything . . .

. . . but the boundaries of it are never clear-cut.

Data is everywhere around you. You can count anything. Dollars in your pocket. Wrinkles in your brow. Amount of happiness in your life. But counting and evaluating aren't always clear-cut. What if you have a credit card in your pocket? How do you count *those* dollars? What counts as a wrinkle? Does it count if it appears only when I furrow my brow?

What about emotions? Are there different kinds of happy? Is my happy the same as yours? Does it matter? It does! The mapmaker's choice about what to include or omit, or where to put the boundaries of the data, is their bias.

What about big data?

Those who have always nodded their way through conversations that included talk of "big data" know that it simply means a lot of data. A *lot* lot. Massive amounts. Big data is a bit of a buzzword because as our computing power has increased, our ability to gather, store, and work with larger and larger data sets has expanded. When you have the ability to run all sorts of calculations on huge amounts of data fairly quickly, you have a new lens on it. You can see new patterns, new possibilities in the world. For some scenarios, big data is necessary and neat.

A map created using big data is, of course, still subject to the intersection of data, bias, and craft. In fact, bias and craft become even more important as the size of the data set increases. Bigger data often means that fancy, opaque algorithms are used to analyze it, and sophisticated graphics programs generate visualizations of it. When something is bigger, fancier, and more polished, it feels more established, more certain to viewers. It can feel more true, but that's not necessarily the case.

If a new friend invites you over for the first time and you pull up and realize they live in a mansion with manicured grounds, you might feel a little intimidated, but you wouldn't think they were a better person just because they had big fancy things. It's the same with big data.

DATA
collection
selection
organization

Allow yourself the somewhat anxious, intimidated "Wow!" but then move on and evaluate the map in the same way you would evaluate one drawn by hand.

Data's raw materials

There are three particular elements to pay attention to with data: how it was collected, how it was selected, and how it is organized.

How was the data collected?

The way data is collected sets the first constraints on the eventual map. When snow falls, it doesn't fall evenly everywhere. So on a map of snowfall in a town, a measurement of snow depth on the east side of town may differ from the depth on the west side. But if only one data point is collected, we'll never know. More data points equal more resolution.

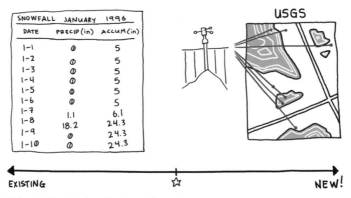

Data might exist already or be collected anew.

But who collected the data, and using what totals? Is it from one weather station run by a local elementary school? A massive automated network? Radar? Interviews with neighbors? A random cross-section of people from town? One person out on their own with a yardstick?

What was the method for doing it? Was it derived from an existing data set or made just for this graphic?

With an existing data set, the creator is tied to what was collected and how it was collected. The boundaries of the set are beyond their control. Their hands are tied a bit, but there is convenience in using something that might take an outsized amount of time or resources to do on their own. The data on snowfall shown here might have been mined from a historical chart of snowfall all across New England.

With a new data set, the mapmaker has the option to collect exactly what they want in a fashion that works for them. They pick the rows and columns and the specific items that were recorded and how. The mapmaker can set the weather stations out and make years of meticulous measurements.

Or maybe the data set is somewhere in between—inspired by or built on something existing, with new information gathered to customize it. Maybe the historical weather data set gave a baseline—a starting point to evaluate the data—and the mapmaker made extra measurements to boost the resolution of the data because they had a hunch that the snow depth varied wildly across town. Bias!

MEANS OF DATA COLLECTION

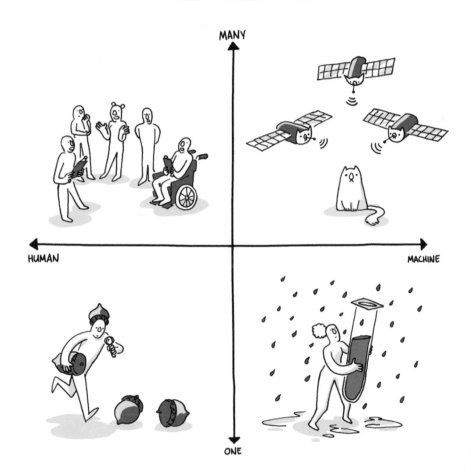

MANY

HUMAN

MACHINE

ONE

In the same way that data can be qualitative or quantitative, the methods used to collect data can be mechanized or human-powered. Note, human-collected doesn't necessarily mean qualitative, and vice versa. A machine could scour Twitter and build a huge qualitative data set. A human can set a grid on a coral reef and hand count the number of bleached corals in each grid-square. Humans and machines can work in groups, too. Teams of humans can do qualitative interviews across a school. Arrays of satellites can track the real-time position of your cat.

Some data collection techniques are simple. Others outrageous. When deconstructing a map, try to understand the method used and the intent behind it.

How was the data selected?

Once data is collected, we need to make meaning out of it. Humans decide what data to use and what to ignore. They select what's out of bounds. They decide how to combine variables and figure out what's interesting. Data boundaries could mimic those in real life—the town limits are where the data ends. Or they might be more arbitrary—say, precipitation under a centimeter is counted as zero. Data sets need consistency.

If this is the chart collected at one specific location . . .

DATE	PRECIPITATION
1/6	1"
Jan. 7	Some snow
January 8	no
1-9	0.8 cm

. . . the actual data set used needs to be cleaned and selected:

DATE	PRECIPITATION
1-6	2.54 cm
1-7	VOID
1-8	0.00 cm
1-9	0.80 cm

Dates and measurements need to be consistent. On January 7, the precipitation value of "some snow" doesn't translate. On the eventual map, the mapmaker needs to decide what values to show, and how; what to include and what to leave out.

How is the data organized?

Your head might see "organized" and immediately think about craft. This isn't wrong, but remember there's an overlap between data and craft. If craft is the map's skin, data is the bones. The portion of map organization that is highly dependent on the data bones is the "base framework." A base framework is the way that the data is laid out on the map. Is it a pie chart? Geographic? A bar chart? A symbol repetition? Different types of base framework are used to highlight different things the creator wants the viewer to notice.

Deconstruct with a focus on data

Marion found a simple bar chart that shows the sugar content of maple syrup, Tang, Coke, milk, and Gatorade. If you first deconstruct it, you can then zoom in on the mapmaker's data decisions.

So, what does the creator of the map want this data to mean?

How was it collected? Probably from information available online or on product labels. It would be easy to verify these numbers.

THE SUGAR BAR DECONSTRUCTION

WHICH EMOTIONS? → PLAYFUL / CONFUSED

WHY THOSE FEELINGS? → LOLLIPOPS / Who cares about this?

HOW IS THAT HAPPENING? → not for marks / Foods chosen are old and new and not all drinks.

How was it selected? Unsure. Why were these five things chosen? All are drinks except for the maple syrup, so the comparison is confusing. Common drinks like juice are missing. There's a mix of dated (Tang) and more recently popular (Gatorade) beverages, so it's hard to know why these specific data points were chosen.

How is it organized? It's a bar chart. Very simple.

More than anything, the data selection stands out. The creator wants us to notice that maple syrup has much more sugar per fluid ounce than any of the beverages. The data selection was a vessel for the creator's bias.

COMMON BASE FRAMEWORKS

AMOUNT / RELATIVE VALUE

BAR CHART

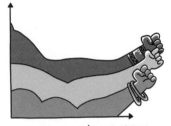

LINE GRAPH / AREA GRAPH

ICON REPETITION

ICON COUNT

These are some of the most common bones of a map. Of course, there are other base frameworks, and many ways to alter any of these.

The same data can be presented using a number of different base frameworks. Pay particular attention to continua. I bet you can find a continuum in almost every map.

PIE / DONUT CHART

RELATIVE SIZE CHART

FILLED ICON

NESTED ICONS

RELATIONSHIP / TENSION

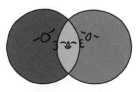

VENN DIAGRAM

CONTINUUM

No limp data!

Have you seen this bumper sticker around town?

Limp data is exactly what it sounds like. For one reason or another, it doesn't stand up. It might be that it was collected poorly or selectively. It might be that it was misinterpreted. It might be that it's represented in a twisted way. Limp data is incomplete in some way.

What does limp data look like? Feel like? Sound like? Is it always obvious, or does it hide in plain sight?

The Tom Burke election flier is limp data.

Are the scholarship and dropout relationships linear? These numbers are according to whom? How was the data collected? We don't know. Selected? Also unknown. Organized? Poorly, using a deceptive base framework. The visual implies the two lines are related, but there is no evidence of connection. This is limp data being used to manipulate the viewer. Limp data and manipulation often go hand in hand.

The sugar content graph might also be accused of containing limp data. On one hand, the selection of maple syrup, Tang, Coke, milk, and Gatorade feels wonky. Maple syrup isn't a beverage (hopefully), but it's compared against a suite of beverages. The data selection is suspect. On the other hand, the sugar values are readily available for anyone who wants to verify them, the presentation is a straightforward bar chart, and the choice to include maple syrup may be more about the mapmaker's agenda than data selection. There might be a message in this map, or maybe it's made to manipulate. If anything about the collection, selection, or organization of data raises eyebrows, you might have a case of limp data. Look out for it in the maps you view—and the maps you make.

CHAPTER XII

It was 10 p.m. Marion knew it was late; still, here she was, knocking at Ms. Turlock's front door. There were holiday candles lit in the windows, even though it was the middle of summer. Odd. The house was Cape Cod style, a compact box with a peaked roof, white with red shutters. These houses used to be the norm around here, but this one looked like a relic—saved from the mini-mansionization of seemingly every other place in this part of town.

Ms. Turlock opened the door. She gestured for Marion to come in, then shuffled toward the living room. Marion followed. The walls were covered with artwork. Paintings mostly, some photographs. All local scenes. All winter-themed.

"I'll make you a mug of hot cocoa." Ms. Turlock walked out. It wasn't a question. It was also a seventy-degree summer night.

Marion stood and looked at all of the art. Downtown covered in snow, lights aglow. Many images of the woods. The school. Marion stepped closer. It was Burke High, but in the painting the name of the school was changed to "Shaw High." A painting of the intersection of Mass Ave. and Burke Road was labeled as "Mass Ave." and "Shaw Rd." Ms. Turlock had rebranded the town and set it in a perpetual winter. Every Burke was now a Shaw.

"Ms. Turlock," Marion called out, "you sure do love winter."

"I do. Winter is the only time when you are in charge," she called from the kitchen. Her voice was cheery.

Marion knew that sentence wasn't Ms. Turlock's own. Why was she quoting Julie?

"Ms. Turlock?" Marion asked tentatively.

"Here you go, honey. Don't scald yourself now. I wouldn't want *you* getting hurt." It smelled like she had scorched the milk.

It was time to get to the point of her visit. "How do you know about the Burkes and Bernadette Shaw? Are you in danger? Is the Burke family threatening you?"

Ms. Turlock sighed and stared at Marion. When she spoke, her voice was calm and direct. "I've been the front office secretary at Burke High for forty-two years. I've been through eight principals, almost nine thousand students, and all that in parents, too. You might think sitting in that chair of mine would get boring, or make someone go mad, but after you stare at something long enough, you start to notice things that wouldn't make anyone else blink. The only thing with a longer tenure at Burke High than me is the Burke family itself.

"And they are a force. There is always some Burke that has some opinion about something. A recommendation for every administrator. A question for the principal. They practically run the school. Fortunately, people like the Burkes tend to let their self-importance haze their peripheral vision, and they forget to notice flowery things on the edges, like front office secretaries." Ms. Turlock gestured at her flower-print shirt.

Then her voice rose and her words came out faster. "They control this town. They have for centuries. Sure, there's some good there. They try and tell themselves that they do more good than harm with what they have, but that doesn't count if all the buds don't get to bloom."

"Has Robby been threatening you?" Marion asked.

"Robby's the worst of them! I told him all about his family, and he goes and tells them! He keeps trying to scare me, but I won't be intimidated. I'm done with that."

She gazed out the back window, then continued, "I even found the epitaph. But proof has eluded me. I saw it once. Yes, I did. Pored over every last detail for the short time I had it, but—well, I think you can find it."

"The epitaph?"

"Oh, Marion. If I'd known you would be this difficult, I would have picked someone else. Well, I did, but that didn't work either."

"Picked me for what? To out the Burkes? To find the proof?"

"I'm tired."

"I'm confused, Ms. Turlock."

"As you are now, so once was I. Goodnight, Marion." Ms. Turlock walked to the door and held it open to the humid night.

CHAPTER XIII

Marion taped up all of her evidence on the wall. USGS map. Hand-drawn woods map. Senses map and Julie's writing—those two went together. Sugar content chart. Woods photo. Picture of the scholar-ship winners. The election poster. A rough chart she'd made using the scholarship winner data and prize money. The Burke family tree. Sticky notes for things that stood out. Bernadette Shaw. The "guilt money" that Robby had talked about in the library. And some evidence came just from her own notes. The letter and poem from Rufus Burke that mentioned Bernadette Shaw—the one Emily remembered being mixed in with the stolen tests. Everything she had just learned from Ms. Turlock.

There had to be something here. She made notes about why each item was interesting, what clues it generated, what questions it raised. She put up blank sheets and began drawing diagrams, forcing herself to find connections. She could do this. It all had to be connected.

The Burkes' problematic legacy and Bernadette Shaw—if it was true, where was the proof? Was it in the Rufus Burke letter? Did Julie actually return it that night? Was this mysterious letter the link to her friend's murder? If she exposed the Burkes, could she also find out what had happened to Julie?

CHAPTER XIV

"Sorry for this, Bernadette."

Marion had taken the longer route to the clearing where Bernadette Shaw's grave lay shrouded in the tall grass. It was 6:30 in the morning and she was already sticky with sweat. She'd had to walk downhill before coming up, and she moved slowly, looking at the map along the way. She'd passed the creek and the burn pit with its now-scattered stones—and then she had an idea.

One by one she moved aside the stones piled on the grave. There were at least forty of them, and she felt bad for disturbing a resting place, but for a grave from 1775, this pile didn't look old enough. It took a few minutes to move all of them.

She brushed the dirt aside, and there it was, almost entirely embedded, flat on the ground. She wiped the soil from the old, thin flagstone. The hand-carved letters were weathered indentations, but still readable.

In memory of Bernadette Shaw
who died Apr. 20, 1775, aged 30 years.
Behold all you that passeth by,
As you are now so once was I,
As I am now so you must be
Prepare for death and follow me.

She didn't have long to consider it.

"Marion!"

Robby was jogging toward her.

The last thing she wanted was to be alone with him in the woods, early in the morning. She wasn't sure what he or his family was mixed up in.

Marion took off through the trees. She had a fifty-yard lead on him. She'd never make it to her car fast enough, but there was one place in the woods where she could hide.

He shouted from the top of the hill, "Marion! I'm here to help you! Why are you running?"

She'd made it to the mossy spot before he could see her duck down. He was still far away.

"It's not what you think!" he called. "We have to do this together! I can protect you!"

Marion had heard him deliver that same line when he thought he was talking to Ms. Turlock in the library. Enough crouching and hiding. She stepped out and stood tall. "Robby—enough! I'm not going to let you intimidate me out of this. Your family is a lie. You are threatening Ms. Turlock for making it known. And you made Julie disappear. You killed her for finding the proof. She was going to expose you, and you killed her!"

There. She'd said what she knew.

There was a pause. His posture sagged. He looked defeated.

"Marion, no. I—*run!*" he shouted.

BANG! Robby fell to the ground.

Marion stood in shock for only a second. Then she turned and ran. She had no idea where the bullet had come from—her only thought was to go so fast that no bullet could find her.

◆ ◆ ◆

Back at home, she stared at her wall of evidence. Robby had been shot. Why? This made no sense. Did the shooter see her? She didn't have much time. She had to figure this out quickly or else she could be next.

The Rufus Burke letter that Emily and Julie had found in the tests—that must be the proof Ms. Turlock was talking about. Julie, instead of returning it with the tests, must have shown it to someone else.

She might have shown it to Robby. He was the one Burke she knew. Or she might have shown it to Ms. Turlock. She was always a confidant.

Of course, Emily also knew it existed. And every time Marion talked to Emily she realized there were more layers to her personality.

Who was motivated to gain possession of that letter? Who wanted that letter so much that they would kill Julie if she didn't want to hand it over? If she wanted to do the honorable thing and turn it in?

Who had something to lose? Something to gain? Robby had already parted from his family trajectory by picking a path that wasn't law. He had nothing to lose, but would he have anything to gain? Not really.

Emily and Ms. Turlock, though—Emily could have wanted to sell the document. She didn't feel bad about stealing and making some money. Why not from something old with value? Ms. Turlock could have seen it as a ticket to gain entry to the Burke way of life. If she could prove that Bernadette Shaw was killed by Rufus Burke, the Burke family might crumble. They'd want to avoid losing their power. With the proof, she'd have leverage with them. Did she have anything to lose by not having the letter? *Her sanity*, Marion thought.

CHAPTER XV

Marion entered Emily's house through a first-floor window. She knocked over thirty tchotchkes in the process, but there wasn't time to be subtle. She took in the room around her, then moved to the next and found what she was looking for. In the corner were Julie's original things. A ceramic penguin, five paper cranes. Three coasters made of geodes. A small wooden box with a frog carved on the lid. She opened everything that had a cover. Looked behind every picture. Slid open each drawer. Shook out each book. Tiny polished rocks came out of a velvet bag. A pile of fortune cookie messages popped out of a horse-shaped jar. Julie's journal, stuffed with notes, some from Marion; newspaper clippings; doodles of words and song lyrics. Marion lifted the journal and confetti fluttered down. Then a box of Nag Champa incense. The woodsy smell was still potent twenty-five years later. She opened the box. There it was. She slid out the paper that was rolled up inside. A letter from Rufus Burke dated 1799, with a poem.

TWO

The Exposé

Figure it out, then share it out proudly.

How do you make a map?

If you want to build an engine, a toaster, or a camera, but you have no idea how they work, you could take apart an existing one to get a sense for each component—what they do, how they fit together, where you have room to try something new, and so on. Armed with that knowledge, some tools and equipment, and some practice, you could build something great. It's the same with maps. In part one we deconstructed them through the lenses of data, bias, and craft. Part two is about using these same levers to create and use maps.

Exploration before explanation

Real talk: nobody knows what they're doing at the beginning of anything.

First time making a salad? What tastes good together?

First time commuting to a new job? What route is best for you?

First time at a P!nk concert? What outfit is going to bring out your inner warrior?

First time making a new map? What should it be about? What data should you use? What base framework makes it most interesting? How should it look if you want it to dazzle the most people?

Before you decide on teal spandex and a scrunchie for that concert, experiment with five other outfits. Before you spend weeks learning graphics programs to make a plot for your next presentation, experiment with the type of data you're using, the way it's presented, and the point of view you're trying to get across.

Taking a moment to look at your data in a new way or generate ideas—is a good reason to make a map. Sometimes that's all the reason you need. Yet many maps are made to explain something to other people. That's good, too. But take a moment to explore before you explain. Exploring takes time, and you are likely eager to jump ahead and make a final draft already, but hold off on eating the marshmallows. Get some inspiration. Allow your brain and body to wander away a bit before you call them home. The most interesting maps are created by people who took the time to explore. Be interesting!

You have to try on multiple outfits to find the one that looks best.

EXPLORE ←———————————————————————→ EXPLAIN

EXPLORE BEFORE YOU EXPLAIN

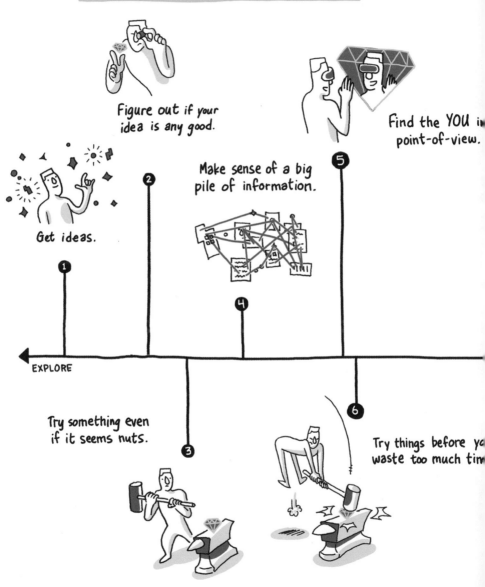

Figure out if your idea is any good.

Find the YOU i point-of-view.

Get ideas.

Make sense of a big pile of information.

Try something even if it seems nuts.

Try things before yo waste too much tim

EXPLORE

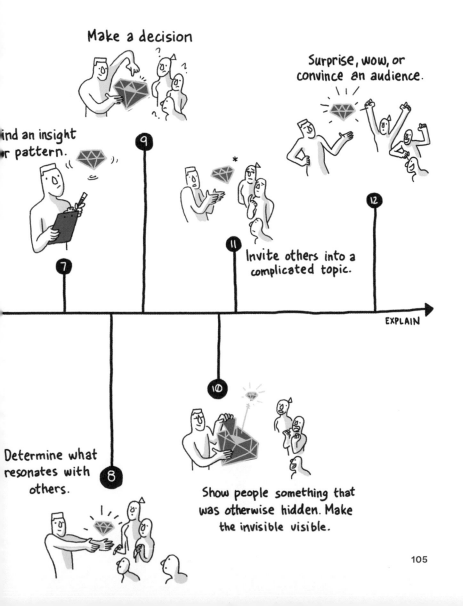

Make a decision

Surprise, wow, or convince an audience.

Find an insight or pattern.

Invite others into a complicated topic.

EXPLAIN

Determine what resonates with others.

Show people something that was otherwise hidden. Make the invisible visible.

Where and how to start exploring?

Surprise! There are three good ways into exploration—
data, bias, and craft. You get to choose where to begin.
Pick a favorite or see if one of these types of corresponding
feelings resonates, and go from there:

Data

I have some data. I want to do something with it.
How do I figure out the most intriguing way to plot it?

Bias

I have a point I want to make. What is the most compelling
way to share it?

Craft

I've always wanted to drop thousands of leaflets from
a hot air balloon over a city and watch them flutter into the
hands of the waiting masses. What cool map should I put
on those papers?

If you relate to one of these feelings, use that as your
starting point. If you're unsure, choose data. There's nothing
better about starting with data over bias and craft, but this
way you don't use your time worrying about starting in
the right spot; instead, you just start. Now start exploring.

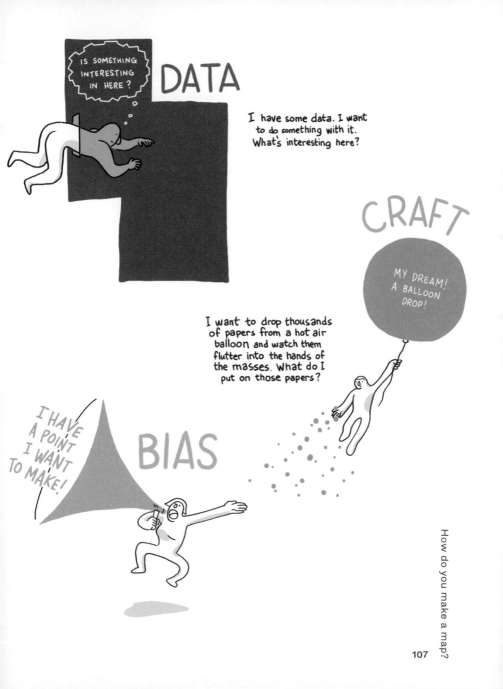

Data Exploration
Knead the dough

So you think you've got a data set. This data set can be anything you've gathered about the subject of your map. It might be an existing mass of numbers available publicly online or the handwritten notes you've collected from a series of interactions with people you suspect committed a crime. It might be a bunch of ideas in your head. It might be a mix of all of these. To find meaning in the data, follow these steps.

In practice, this is organic and messy. This is how you look at your data through multiple lenses. Here's Marion's investigation of all of her current data and ideas about Julie's murder.

1 **Gather the data you have.**

For Marion, this means:

Any notes and observations she's scribbled down based on conversations with Emily, Ms. Turlock, and Robby.

Observations and notes about different places. like their homes and the woods.

Pieces of evidence she's found, like the maps hidden behind the woods photos and paintings.

Items she's gathered, like the spreadsheet of scholarship amounts and winners and Tom Burke's election poster.

2 **Highlight (literally) the interesting things in your notes.** Get ideas out of your head and onto paper.

For Marion, this means:

Highlighting the items that stand out.

Making sure to include observations of anything odd or out of place that might be a lead.

3 **Make your data moveable and modular.** You need to be able to move it around with your fingers in order to work with it. You should print it out and cut it up. Break its current ties so you can find new connections.

For Marion, this means:

Gathering scissors and sticky notes or notecards.

Taking the existing data set of the names of all the 150 scholarship winners from Burke High School, including the year they won their scholarship and the amount of money they received, and printing out the spreadsheet. Each *Name, Date, Amount* combo is one row of data, one module.

Cutting out the rows. Since Marion's data set is large, she picks just a handful—say ten to twenty data points. She's just exploring and needs enough to spark some new ideas.

Making modular piles of her qualitative observations. This means transferring highlighted items from the previous step onto sticky notes or notecards, one item per card.

Grouping piles together based on whatever categories feel relevant. She shouldn't overthink these groups. Marion's are

1. things that she wonders—basically the things she's seen and heard that give her pause, including her questions—and

2. evidence, both found and gathered.

① GATHER
THE DATA

② HIGHLIGHT
INTERESTING
THINGS. GET
THEM OUT OF
YOUR HEAD.

③ MAKE
MODULAR PILES.
ONE THING
PER PAPER.
YOUR CATEGORIES
MAY DIFFER.

THINGS I WONDER

NUMBERS

EVIDENCE I HAVE

MAKES
ME
WONDER

Who killed Julie?

Why?

What are the Burke's covering up?

Why?

Emily is biggest scholarship winn__

Why?

"peripheral deletions"

· Marion + mom
· Emily + Julie
· ____ mossy spot

Is Emily involved?

· Private life + Public Persona very different

Who shot Robby?

Was he hurting or helping Marion?

Why is Ms. Turlock leaving clues?

Marion smells everything

Why is Robby different from his family?

Why does Ms Turlock sneak to Bernadette's grave?

Why does Robby want to pay off Ms. Turlock?

Ms. Turlock's house is stuck in winter

EVIDENCE

WOODS MAP

· Who made this?
· so accurate
· mossy spot missin__

USGS MA__

__arger area
__from woods m__

EPITAPH

Behold all you that passeth by,
As you are now so once was I,
A__ I am now so you mu__
____

RUFUS BURKE CONFESSION

· Why so important to Ms. Turlock
· who knows it exists?

SENSES MAP

· obsessive detail
· seems same hand as woods
· illustrating Julie's writing?

JULIE'S WRITI__

· from literary mag before she disappeared

BURKE FAMILY TREE

· not all names filled
· mostly Burkes's left for Marion to find ____?"

__M BURKE __ELECTION POSTER

__d claims feel misleading
__rke's run for everything

WOODS PHOTO

· from Emily's office
· other things hidden behind

WOODS PAINT__

from Ms Turlock Marion

__mily tree behi__

SUGAR CHART

· Tang included + Ms. Turlock loves Tang
· not sure purpose?

④

MOVE THOSE
PILES TO FIND
MEANING.

Use continua to
begin to explore
which variables
exist.

YOUNG ⟷ OLD

STRUGGLING ⟷ STABLE

LIQUID ⟷ SOLID

Use Venns to
find relationships.

Use nested systems
to expand boundaries
of your data.

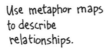

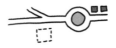

Use metaphor maps
to describe
relationships.

Use 2x2s to
overlay variables
and hunt for
insights.

4 **Experiment with continua, Venn diagrams, nested systems, metaphor maps, and 2×2s to find interesting variables, relationships, and insights in your data.** This is where things get really fun. It's also tricky and takes practice. Essentially, you must let your spirit fingers take over and experiment with putting your data into a series of different groups. To make these groups, use simple base frameworks. Each of these types of frameworks will help illuminate your data in different ways.

With this exercise, you're using maps to find ideas. You are doing data exploration loops. You're not trying to make a rough draft of your final map. Don't get bogged down in thinking about where each map might go. Just search for the sparks—the things that are really interesting. This is your lens switching to see what might come into focus. It's idea sketching. I know it's hard to wrap your head around, and not all of these frameworks will work for you. But if you don't play the state lottery you'll never know if there's $100,000 behind the scratcher. Here's how to experiment with the following base frameworks.

Start with a continuum

Continua are my personal heroes. They are absolutely the most versatile type of map. In every data set, quantitative and qualitative, there is at least one continuum—and often many. If you identify the most interesting ones in your data, you can leverage them into myriad maps.

Draw a nice large continuum—really just a line with points or arrows on each end—on a piece of paper, label the endpoints, and move your data around to see how it lands.

If you're unsure where to begin with your endpoints, start by trying to find a timeline, a tension, and a transition in your data.

For Marion, a timeline might be the ordering of scholarship data based on years (1871 to 2019). This leads to an idea: to order the data using a transition, from low to high monetary values. This helps highlight outlier years, the low lows and high highs. If she thought this was interesting enough to pursue in more detail, she could bring the low/high investigation back to the full data set on the computer. This is a simple example. Yes, I know you could have thought of it without the paper strips, but the thing to pay attention to is the "organize, notice something, reorganize" way of working with data in the analog. These are data exploration loops.

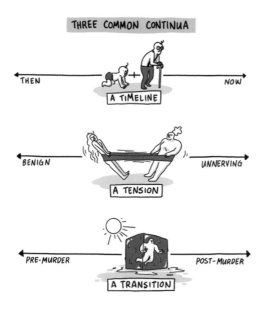

THREE COMMON CONTINUA

THEN — NOW
A TIMELINE

BENIGN — UNNERVING
A TENSION

PRE-MURDER — POST-MURDER
A TRANSITION

You keep going until something pops out. When it does, you might bring that idea back to a computer to analyze your full data set or make a note of it and pursue a different angle.

With qualitative or mixed data, analog continua are even bigger champions. Try using tensions as endpoints, even if you're not quite sure what data would fit where.

In Marion's work, she is wrestling with the tension between good and evil. One or more people did something horrible. Other people are good. There's also a tension between the haves and the have-nots. The people themselves become new data points. The Burke family seems to have everything.

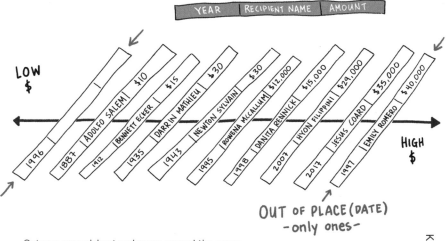

Cut up a spreadsheet and move around the paper.

Ms. Turlock does not. The far edges are easy here, but what about the middle? With Emily and Robby, it's unclear where they fall. Emily's ranking as the highest scholarship winner might put her toward "have," but her sister is dead, so she has lost someone, moving her toward "have-not." Robby is from a wealthy family—a "have"—but he's gone his own way. We don't know why or the surrounding circumstances of his current life. He could be a "have-not." Both of those questions in the middle are interesting to follow up on.

There's also a tension between invisible and visible things. Ms. Turlock feels invisible. She's worked in the background, without recognition, for years, and we know it's eating

away at her. The Burkes are a very visible family. They flaunt their philanthropy, and their family history is the town's history. Rufus Burke is well known as the town hero. And Bernadette Shaw has been erased because of him. That makes her invisible, too. Marion is also invisible. She can't seem to get a handle on life. Where would Emily land? The invisible/visible exploration highlights another tension: that Ms. Turlock is obsessed with the Burkes, but they don't seem to notice her. This could be a clue.

Or maybe it isn't a clue. Each continuum leads to another and another. Make notes along the way. The data points may or may not all fit each time. You might think of a

Knead the dough

continuum that you don't yet have data for and realize you need to do more collection. Some continua will be really interesting. Others will be bland. Allow yourself to explore the stories in the data with your hands.

Let it flow. Lay out a continuum and ask *What questions does this raise?* Write them down. What seems fascinating or unsettling? Write it down. Start with simple endpoints that may even seem too obvious. Don't try to be clever. Timelines are always great beginnings. I know you think you can do this in your head, but you can't. I guarantee that if you actually write it all down, you'll think of an idea that you wouldn't have thought of otherwise.

After you get some of those new ideas, try out some different base frameworks to push your exploration even further. You're exploring for a few reasons. First, you want to find a hook—to figure out what the truly interesting elements are in there. You are also doing it because you want to figure out what data you actually need. This might be very different from what you have now! Remember, each new base framework is a new lens on your information. You're exploring to figure out where to focus. Again, what you try here doesn't determine the eventual shape your final draft will take.

The Venn diagram and its amorphous cousin

Venn diagrams are good for forcing yourself to find relationships between things that might seem unrelated. Start by labeling or putting pieces of your data in the big circles, then focus on figuring out what they have in common. Some will be obvious, and in others the "aha!" will be in the overlaps. Remember, don't try to think and then write. Just write things in the circles, *then* think.

Marion will start with the senses map and Julie's writing from the literary magazine. Both are pieces of evidence. Study them closely. They're about the same topic. That's the overlap. Okay, maybe Marion knew that already, but *why* the senses map exists is a big question. Whoever drew it was really focused on Julie's work for some reason.

SENSES MAP

· obsessive detail
· seems same hand as woods
· illustrating Julie's writing?

JULIE'S WRITING

· from literary mag before she disappeared

SAME TOPIC

Start in the circles and find the overlap

Now try something that seems more difficult: Ms. Turlock in one circle and Julie's writing in the other. Is there a relationship there? Well, Marion has heard Ms. Turlock say, "In winter you are in charge." The exact same line is in Julie's writing. A clue?

Here's another. Marion in one circle and Emily in the other. They were in high school at the same time. They both miss Julie a lot. They also were both around and very much in Julie's life when she went missing. Maybe some of the last people to see her. Another clue?

Venn diagrams are about relationships. Relationships are often about people. People come in many shapes. Sometimes an amorphous Venn is the best way to express

the complicated relationships between people. Draw a Venn, but make the shapes blobby. Include an outlier circle. As with a basic Venn, fill in the main circles, then ask yourself about the overlaps and the outliers. You will learn as you write.

One to try from Marion's investigation might place Ms. Turlock, Marion, and the Burke family in the three large areas. An overlap between Ms. Turlock and the Burkes is the school and scholarship wall she stares at all day. It's all of the Burkes who come and go through her life. An overlap between Ms. Turlock and Marion is the Tang Spot memories and the fact that both of them are now alone. Between Marion and the Burkes there isn't much to go on. They basically coexist. The amorphousness has made a second overlap between Ms. Turlock and the Burkes, though. It's the Rufus Burke confession letter. Ms. Turlock wants it. Does the Burke family want it, too? The overlap between all three of them may be another clue. Marion might be more involved than we know— or even she knows. Perhaps Robby is missing from the diagram. Where does he belong?

The amorphous Venn helps sort through relationships. You could keep going here or try another base framework.

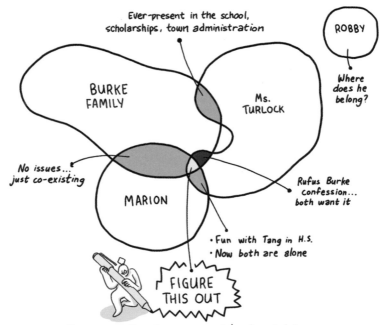

The amorphous Venn gives you more overlaps to search for.

The nested system

Nests are good for expanding your current ideas about the boundaries of your data set. Start by placing one type of data in a middle layer of the nest. Then force your thinking outward—what is a larger container for that kind of data? Force it inward—what is a subset of it? Use as many layers as you need.

For Marion's investigation this might mean placing the "her woods" map in the middle layer of the nest. What's larger than that? There's the literal surrounding area. The USGS map covers this larger area. Julie went missing in a snowy winter. Snowfall in the surrounding area around the time of Julie's disappearance might be of importance. Or look inward, literally. Is Julie buried in the woods? Where? Are there places to dig or hide a body even if it's snowing? The nest helps push your thinking out and in. It helps reshape the possible.

Nested systems work beyond the literal, too. Place the "her woods" map back in the center. What's larger? Well, this map was hidden, along with other documents, behind the woods photograph. Those other things are the larger layer. And the smaller? "Her woods" and all of those hidden documents are all quite sensory. Julie's writing and the senses map are specifically about the senses activated in those woods. The chart about maple

Knead the dough

syrup and Tang, Coke, Gatorade, and milk is about sugar content, but those are all things you taste. The photo is visual. And Marion seems to have a sixth sense about the woods and their depiction in the map. Thinking "sensory" leads to thoughts of each sense, including smell—something that Marion can't help but notice. More clues? You're looping through the data.

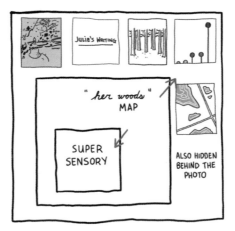

The metaphor map

Metaphor maps help highlight relationships within and among your data. Use them as arbitrary frameworks that you can force data into, seeking an insight. Let's say your data is a solar system: What part of it is the sun? Who orbits whom? Say your data is a river: What is the main fast flow? What are the banks? If your data is a convenience store: What are the different aisles? What's near the cash register?

If we make Marion's investigation a city downtown, what are all the different parts? Draw a simple, generic map of a downtown. Have a main plaza, a main street, some side streets, some buildings, maybe a highway in the distance. The central plaza—the area that everything surrounds—could be the mysterious letter found among the tests that Emily stole. A main road in town could be the "her woods" map. A side street or on-ramp could be the scholarship information. Emily, Robby, and Ms. Turlock each live somewhere. A big question might be who has a second home at the intersection of "her woods" and the scholarship info? Could that be a lead? Important— you're not drawing a literal map of a town. You're using a metaphor to help consider the information you have in a new way. Work the metaphor.

If relationships were a city...

2×2

Use a 2×2 to overlay variables and make insights pop. The 2×2 is the continuum's cousin. Overlay a couple of your continuum ideas and determine what data would fall in each quadrant. Consider what each quadrant represents. Sometimes empty quadrants are the exciting ones. As you fill in the 2×2, you are processing your data. You are making sense of the information you have. A new insight or a story might emerge.

In Marion's investigation, the missing letter from Rufus Burke seems to be a key element. Overlay two continua: *to lose/to gain* and *everything/nothing.* You've created quadrants that can help you think through the motivations

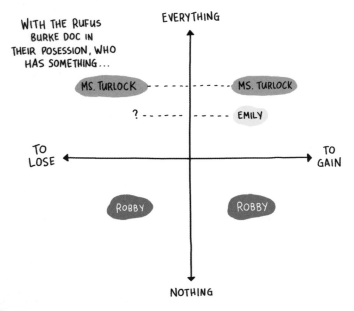

of each character for wanting that letter. With the Rufus Burke document in his possession, Robby really has nothing to lose or nothing to gain. We haven't learned that he wanted to expose his family secret, or even if he knew about it. He's already forged his own path in life. If Emily had the document in 1996, she might have everything to gain. She stole tests for money; it's plausible that she might see it as one more thing she could sell. If Ms. Turlock had the document, she also might have everything to gain. Presumably, she could use it to out the Burke family secret and have Bernadette Shaw's real story—and honor—restored. She could also have a more ulterior motive: wanting to use it to get something from

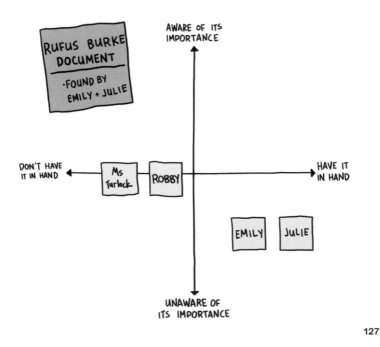

the Burkes. Does she also have everything to lose? She might—if it was taken away. This is a lead to loop into another 2×2.

Still considering the Rufus Burke letter, overlay two continua: *have/don't have it in hand* and *aware/unaware of its importance.*

In 1996, Emily and Julie found the letter. They both saw it and had it in hand. They didn't know it was important. Emily claims that Julie took it along with the stolen tests to return to the school, but it seems that she might have shown it to someone else first. That person could have been Ms. Turlock—we know they were close. Or she could have shown it to Robby, a friend who is also a Burke. So Robby and Ms. Turlock start near the middle. It's unclear whether they have or ever had the letter, and also unclear if they knew how important it was.

Actually, it's the upper right quadrant that has all the power. If someone moves into that quadrant, they can do whatever they want with the document. So who is it? Who did Julie show it to? Did they see value in it and realize its importance?

What would Julie do in that quadrant? She was honorable; she was on her way to return stolen tests. She'd probably return the document to its rightful owner, too.

Emily might sell it. She definitely saw it. But she turned her life around after Julie berated her for the theft. Her motives are a bit muddy.

It's also unclear what Robby might do. He's got nothing to lose or gain by having the letter. He'd learn about his family's false history, but his life didn't hinge on that. He was going his own way.

Again, Ms. Turlock might use it to restore the legacy of Bernadette Shaw. She might also use it for her own gain. We know she's obsessed with the Burkes, to the point of paranoia. She might see it as an opportunity to hold something over them. Being taken for granted by them for so long has contributed to her mania.

Did you find something interesting?

Take the items that stand out and expand on them. Nuggets from the continua, Venn diagrams, and the 2×2s swirl around each character's potential motives. The nested system showed that the area of "her woods" is smaller than the area of the USGS map. It could suggest expanding the scope of your search for a body to a wider area than just the immediate woods, to include more of the surrounding area. The nested system also highlighted the importance of senses.

There are many potential next steps out of data exploration. They might include collecting more data, filtering or performing a new analysis on existing data, or deciding the data you have isn't worth exploring further. Or you may have a big insight now and be ready to move on to explanation, creating the final draft of your map.

Knead the dough

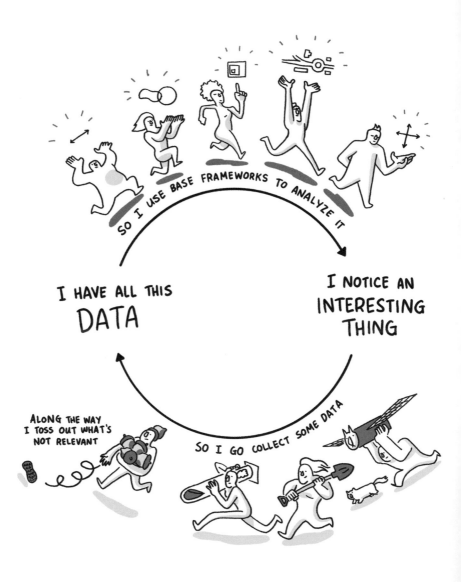

A note on working with big(ish) data sets: Often the interesting trends in a huge data set are visible only when you work with the data on a computer. You need statistics and maybe even machine learning to explore them. Plot different variables against one another, add layers to a geographic map, use a machine-learning algorithm to figure out how different variables might be related. Really do this! This is another way of exploring your data, and you might be more comfortable staying on your machine, but do this in addition to analog manipulation, not instead of it. You'll be surprised how your analog work might inspire your digital discoveries.

Whatever your process, look out for limp data

Now that you've explored your data, it's time to try something else. To choose *bias,* go to page 133. To choose *craft,* go to page 139. To ride into the wind with reckless abandon, go to page 148.

Exploring with data without a data set

Shhhhh. It's okay. You can't solve a murder with no data and no ideas, but you can still quickly get some data and start exploring with all the same frameworks.

List all of the soft things that you can touch right now. Data set!

Keep track of the number of times the person in the cube next to you clears their throat. Data set!

Take a picture every day at 6:06 p.m. Data set!

Grab your online search history data for the last thirty days. Data set!

Go to data.gov and click on a topic that interests you. Data set!

Don't forget that data can be either visible or invisible.

Whew! Data really is everywhere. Feel free to be playful. Tinkering with something that you think is inane can have fascinating results.

Bias Exploration
Agendas are for everyone

You might have an agenda already. You might wish you had one. Or you might want to shift someone's thinking about a certain topic, or want to get your own voice out. Exploring with bias means investigating human behavior, motivations, and values. It means examining the nuances of other people, and it means turning the spotlight inward on yourself. This might manifest in different ways.

If you have an agenda, state it as best you can. You can also fill in an interesting contradiction or something you found surprising. Then list all of the reasons why you think your agenda is important. Also list all of the things you believe are causing this belief. For each of these lists, get even listier and list whatever data you would need in order to investigate further.

For example, imagine you lived in Marion's world, and you wanted to tell the community that the Burkes have too much power and it needs to be curbed. You might think that's an important agenda because the Burkes are living on stolen gains, and honesty is important. You might feel this way to begin with because there are so many Burkes in positions of power in town, and they control the fate of so many students with their scholarships. Those are just opinions, though. To investigate the number of Burkes in power, you need some data on the actual number of them in power. That's a next step. Try to get some of that data. Remember, when you actually have the data, you may end up changing your point of view. Embrace your inner flip-flopper at this point. You're exploring based on bias.

If you have an agenda, unpack it to figure out your next step.

You might start instead with yourself and hold up a mirror to figure out your agenda. Remember, bias can come from either the creator or the viewer. Explore it from both sides.

UNPACK YOUR AGENDA

If you have an audience that you want to impress, and you wish you had an agenda, map that audience. This applies if you're giving a talk, presenting something to a team, or trying to get a community to work together.

Then go and talk with people who are part of that audience. Ask some questions. Ask them to tell you a story about a specific topic. Figure out what is really interesting to them, notice tensions or contradictions in what they say,

MAP YOUR AUDIENCE

WHO ARE THEY?

WHAT IS IMPORTANT TO THEM?

WHY DO THEY CARE ABOUT THIS?

WHAT DO YOU WANT THEM TO DO? SHIFT THEIR THINKING? EXPLORE?

HOW DO YOU WANT THEM TO FEEL?

WHERE MIGHT YOU GO TO INTERACT WITH THEM? → WHAT WOULD YOU ASK? → WHY IS THAT INTERESTING?

DO YOU KNOW WHAT CULTURES OR GROUPS ARE THEY A PART OF?

and make note of these. Begin to collect data based on those observations.

Map out who you are and what motivates you. You're acknowledging the biases you bring to the project. Next, select a topic, any topic. Pick the top story in today's paper. Also look at all you've articulated about who

MAP YOURSELF

WHO ARE YOU?

WHAT'S IMPORTANT TO YOU?

HOW DO YOU IDENTIFY? WHATEVER THAT MEANS TO YOU?

You

WHAT PARTS OF YOU DO YOU WANT TO COME THROUGH?

WHAT CULTURES OR GROUPS ARE YOU PART OF?

PICK A NEWS HEADLINE. WHAT'S YOUR LENS ON THAT STORY?

WHAT DO YOU WANT TO HIDE?

Agendas are for everyone

you are, how you identify, and what you believe in. What's your lens on the story? How do you react to it? Collect some data based on your answers.

A strong agenda is an excellent starting point for a map. With it you can collect the data that will express your story. You can figure out what shapes your map might take and where it needs to be placed to be most effective. If you don't consider your bias, you're putting all of that responsibility on the viewer. If you can't articulate the point of your map in one or two sentences, how is your audience supposed to understand it? A map with no point is sloppy and inconsiderate. You're not either of those, so take a few minutes and hone your agenda.

Craft Exploration
Shape shift

Sometimes you get a song stuck in your head. No matter what you do, you just keep hearing that song over and over and over and over, and the only thing that helps get it out is doing something totally different. Maybe you go out for a drink with an old friend or go for a walk in the woods. Sometimes you get an idea stuck in your head, or you're stuck and can't crack the case. You need another way to think about things—a different way to work through problems and ideas. Exploring with craft is just that. It's about getting your hand moving in order to get your brain grooving.

When you have mapmaker's block, do a craft exploration. Use your own crazy visions, lame doodles, and the physical world right around you to zap your brain into a new creative space.

When you lead with craft, it might not feel like a map is just around the corner. But *it is.* The thing with all of these exercises is that they work only if you do them. Pen to paper. The brain-to-body connection is critical. They won't work as thought exercises.

Balloon drops and other big visions

Sometimes, you know how you want to express a big vision, but you don't know what to show with it. If you recall, I, too, have always wanted to release thousands of fliers from a hot air balloon. That hot air balloon is the form and the context that I know I want to use, even though I don't know what I'm going to do with it yet. Your form might be a simple scatter plot or crazy concentric circles. Your context might be the local coffee shop or a company all-hands meeting. You pick. After you choose, dissect the elements of those choices as a way to explore with craft. It's okay if you have a big crazy vision that doesn't feel like it has anything to do with maps.

First, draw your scene. Then label three to five elements of the scene and list why you like each one. Why is it compelling? Is it the huge size of the balloon that feels like an opportunity to make a big statement? Is it the way that the cloud of paper fliers would flutter through the air? Is it that thousands of people would be looking at the same words on those pieces of paper, all at once? Is it that you, up there in the sky, would feel all-powerful? Maybe it's a combination of a few things. Then expand on each of your labels. What type of information would be great conveyed in that way? What data would you need for it?

This might lead you right to a next step to help achieve this big vision—or maybe you need to acknowledge that hot air balloon propaganda drops are beyond your budget. If the latter is the case, add one more layer to your scene dissection: *What are all the* other *ways I could achieve that feeling or that moment?* Do a mini brainstorm on each of those, and then move on to collecting some data.

This works for any context and any form, even if you don't yet have a topic. Always wanted to make a chart full of spirals? Draw it and dissect it. Feel like a simple bar chart would be super satisfying? Go for it.

If you don't have a strong pull toward a form that you want to try, pick something random and make that your canvas. What's right in front of you? Use it as inspiration. There's a water bottle on my desk. It's interesting that it's curved and you can't see all sides of it at once. What kinds of information might be neat to reveal slowly? What would benefit from the slow reveal of spinning it around in your hand? Are there other ways to get a slow reveal?

Little visions (people with no vision welcome, too)

Sometimes you really can't get going. You have zero ideas. Negative vision. You need some warm-up inspiration. If this is you, start by making some marks. Draw a square, an uneven oval, or some lines, or repurpose a coffee stain.

Now you've made some marks. Use them to inspire some next steps. With your square, write your pet peeve in the center and on each side write some type of data you could collect to tally that pet peeve.

With your uneven oval, write a strongly held belief of yours in the middle and make a mind map out of it. Free-associate. What are all the components of that belief? Subcomponents. You're diving into bias.

Like seeing an animal in the clouds, what does that coffee stain look like? See an image in it. What kind of map might you make based on that image?

With any of these exercises, you're working with hunches and imaginary information. But you're making something. You're forming connections between your head and hand. You're doing a free-write before you write the novel.

OF PAPER CRINKLES
IN THE MOVIE THEATER

PET PEEVE:

LOUD
EATERS

OF GUM
CLICKS PER
MINUTE FROM
LADY NEXT
TO ME

TIMES GUY
AT WORK SAYS
"MMM" AFTER
EACH BITE

OF TIMES I MOVE TO
GET AWAY FROM A
LOUD EATER

UNPACKING BALLOON DROPS
& OTHER BIG VISIONS

I LIKE THIS BECAUSE:

WHAT TYPE OF INFO WOULD BE GREAT IF DISPLAYED THIS WAY?

• I could make a huge statement.

• Simple
• Color
• Might be hard to read a map from the ground

• Everyone feels a sense of camaraderie.

• Anticipation excites people

• They will all focus on understanding the map.

• Something that's very of the moment.

WHAT TYPE OF DATA FITS THIS DESCRIPTION?

WHAT OTHER FORM FACTORS MIGHT HELP ACHIEVE SOME OF THESE FEELINGS

• Map could be the paper wrapper on everyone's sandwich

• Map could be texted en masse at the same time

• Map could be...
ANYTHING!

• Could announce election results, or winners of a different contest.

Get physical

Use the real world as inspiration for both what you map and how you map it. Take a handheld object, like a jar of Tang. If you had to make a map of something related to Tang that was relevant to you, what might you measure? Maybe you could record how often you use it or go through a jar. If you had to visualize this map using jars of Tang, it might look like this:

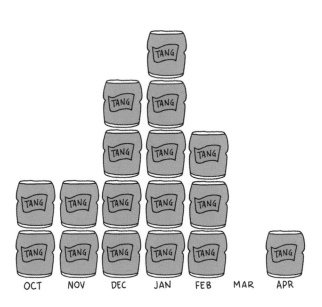

Or think about the topic you want to explore, and select a physical object that is related to it. Pick it up or walk around it. Experience it in the real world. Don't just think about it. Actually interacting with it might trigger an idea for how and what you want to share about it.

You can find ways to interact with invisible things, too. Smells are invisible, but they're from the real world. Get your nose up close to a smell, take a big sniff, and then sketch it—whatever that means. Do this for all the smells that stand out. Figure out what they have in common or where they intersect and overlap with each other.

If you were Marion, you might overlay those smells on a map of the woods. Looking at them on top of a geography could be a clue.

Your craft explorations might trigger an idea that you want to explore and inspire a type of data to collect. Do it! Or maybe you've discovered an audience you want to convince, or you still need an agenda and you should now explore with bias. You will need to swirl around in your exploration of data, bias, and craft for a while before you're ready to move on. It'll feel slow. You'll think you're ready to start making the final draft before you actually are, and you'll jump ahead anyway, but that's okay. When that final draft isn't working and you feel out of sorts because you don't know why, you can always come back and explore.

Shape shift

Explain all day

Each time you explore with data, bias, or craft, you move yourself down the continuum toward explanation. You know you're ready to explain when you have your data, know why it's interesting, know what story you want to tell, and have a sense for what form factor you want your map to take. Now it's time to make the map that you want other people to see.

When other people see your work, they're going to deconstruct it. Everything you learned about deconstructing for data, bias, and craft applies as you build.

EXPLORE

Pay particular attention to craft's raw materials. How it's made is what it means. Bias will always find its way into what you make. It will also show up in how people receive it. We don't easily separate from ourselves. It's critical to pay attention to how you collect, select, and organize your data. Enough of it may or may not be enough.

Make a sketch of your final map. This is the first draft of what you want to show to the world.

Now, even though you think you know exactly what you want to show in your map and how, there's always room to push it further. Exploration to explanation is a continuum, after all. Here are a few more things for you to experiment with to help refine your maps and their meanings.

DATA SET

STORY I WANT TO TELL

FORM FACTOR IDEA

EXPLAIN

Base framework flop

Much as you used different base frameworks to look for patterns within your data, you can try different base frameworks to express your data, too. For example, going from a bar chart to relative size chart for the sugar content plot gives the map a different feel.

MAPLE SYRUP
13.4 g/tbsp

TANG
1.8

COKE
1.6

MILK
0.8

GATORADE
0.4

The bar chart version shows the sugar comparison, but the spoon version allows you to feel it. We all have a sense for the size of a sugar cube.

Continua like to mingle

Secret mapping trick: Take data that you have in a continuum, and combine it with data you have in a different type of base framework. This is how people make more sophisticated maps. The multiplication might make you calculate a new variable or collect a new data value.

Obviously, they're not perfect multiplications, but the act of forcing the combination will help you craft a more nuanced, more data-laden map.

JUMPING JACKIES

CONTINUUM x BAR CHART

DISTANCE JUMPED
RELATIVE TO
BODY HEIGHT

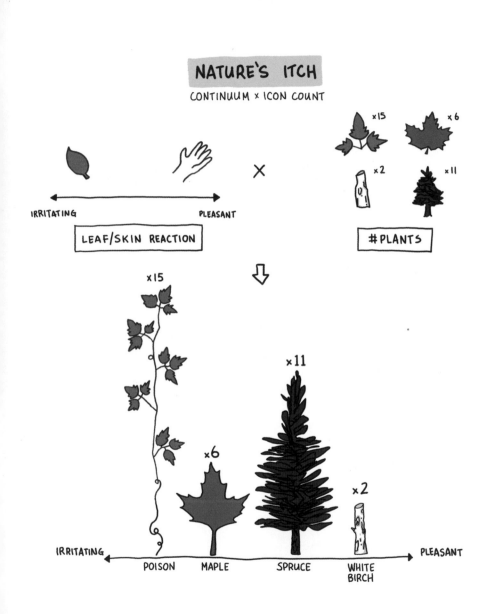

NATURE'S ITCH

CONTINUUM × ICON COUNT

×15 ×6 ×2 ×11

LEAF/SKIN REACTION

IRRITATING   PLEASANT

×

#PLANTS

×15

×11

×6

×2

IRRITATING   PLEASANT

POISON   MAPLE   SPRUCE   WHITE BIRCH

TASTEBUD TANGO

CONTINUUM x CONTINUUM

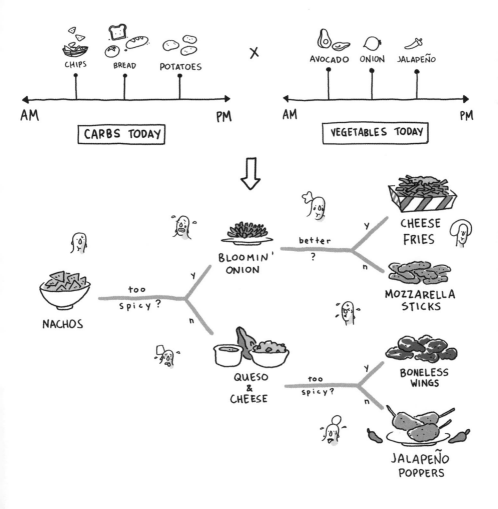

CHIPS · BREAD · POTATOES

AM — PM

CARBS TODAY

X

AVOCADO · ONION · JALAPEÑO

AM — PM

VEGETABLES TODAY

NACHOS

too spicy?

y → BLOOMIN' ONION

better? → y → CHEESE FRIES

n → MOZZARELLA STICKS

n → QUESO & CHEESE

too spicy? → y → BONELESS WINGS

n → JALAPEÑO POPPERS

WHAT IF YOUR PROJECT WAS...

REVEALED BY TOUCH OR SOUND?
PLAY WITH SENSES

EXPERIENCED FROM ALL ANGLES?
GO 3D

REVEALED BY REMOVING LAYERS?
PLAY WITH TIME

NESTED, LIKE RUSSIAN DOLLS?
PLAY WITH TIME

BIGGER THAN YOU?
PLAY WITH SCALE

WEARABLE?
GO 3D

HELD IN ONE HAND?
PLAY WITH SCALE

EXPERIENCED BY LOOKING OR CRAWLING INSIDE SOMETHING?
GO 3D

154

Form factor switch-up

If you're not sure whether you look good, you might try on another outfit. If you're concerned that your map isn't quite right, you might try on a new form factor.

Experiment with making the same point with the same data in three entirely different form factors. Close your eyes and let your finger land somewhere on the page. Create in the form factor you land on.

Reality to representation explosion

If you're feeling like your visual lacks personality or pizzazz, think about shifting to a unique graphic shape to represent your data. Recall that a bar chart made of bars is just that, and one made of raised hands adds a layer of meaning. The same holds true for any type of map.

Start by writing down the actual data you are representing. Let's say it's oranges. Then, challenge yourself to come up with as many different ways to represent oranges as possible. You might sketch a picture of a whole orange, an orange wedge, slice, or curled piece of the rind. Maybe you could use orange trees. Grab an actual orange, then zoom in and use the orange texture. Sketch it. Keep going and think about objects that are commonly associated with oranges, like juicers or cartons or glasses of juice. Think about rituals that involve them, like breakfast. Think about states or countries where oranges are popular and draw their outlines. Consider quotes, pop-culture, and orange products like Orangina, Tang, or Tropicana. Draw sketches of all of these and more as a way to force yourself to find a new way to represent your data. This will ultimately enhance the craft of your map.

REWORD YOUR TITLE TO CHANGE THE VIBE

COVER OF TABLOID

GRANDMA'S RECIPE

PERSONALITY QUIZ

SCIENTIFIC PAPER

PROTEST MARCH POSTER

HUMOR MAGAZINE

Vibe check

Vibe is the aura that your map gives off. It changes the way that people feel about it. If your map's vibe feels off, ask one of those friends who will be honest with you to tell you what vibe, what attitude, what personality your map exudes. Does it match up with the vibe you are trying to communicate? Have you forgotten to consider a vibe? It's not too late! Is it witty or sarcastic? Is it compassionate? Matter of fact? Remember that your words can have a huge impact on your vibe. Try rewording your title with a new vibe. Watch how it changes your maps.

Don't forget the details

You wouldn't invest a bunch of money in a beautiful painting and then put it up on your wall and leave it hanging crooked. Don't do that with your maps, either. Make sure you take care of the final details.

Hang them straight. Or the digital equivalent: don't alter the aspect ratio as you size them to fit your screens.

Cite your data sources. As appropriate, include how your data was collected and selected. Don't let your data go limp by failing to cite.

Remember to include labels and titles.

State your position. Most maps don't do this, but consider adding a short paragraph about you and your position in an author bio section.

Parting thought

When you're mapmaking, make with intention. Viewers will read meaning into every decision you make. They'll also read meaning into decisions you forget to make. The data you use and how it was collected, selected, and organized are the crux of the map. If your data's gone limp, the map has nothing to stand on. If you're trying to make sense of a lot of data or a complicated scenario, use base frameworks to help evoke your own ideas. When in doubt, map it out.

The point you're trying to make—your agenda—is your bias. It will be interpreted by people with different biases and different life experiences. Your intention may be different from your audience's actual reaction. Thoughtfully consider the bias cloud for the maps you make, and you will tell a great story through your map. Do it poorly, and you may unintentionally offend your viewers.

The craft of your map is the vessel that conveys your ideas to the world. Remember FML CTC: form, material, line, color, text, and context. Every decision matters.

If you ever feel stagnant—maybe your data's gone limp, or the form factor you're using is just too complex—go back and explore with a new starting point.

Maps are special tools. They help us make sense of our world. They answer questions and tell stories. They can highlight inequalities. They can pinpoint motives. A series of maps tied together can form a full story. They can help uncover a crime. A series of maps can shape an exposé.

CHAPTER XVI

◆ *Six months later* ◆

Marion stood in front of a crowd in the library's big community room. The audience overflowed from the chairs into the rest of the library. It felt like the whole town was there to honor Julie and dedicate the space to her. Marion inhaled and thought it smelled right—like damp clothes and justice. She began reading aloud:

> *6 January 1799.*
> *Dearest Family, Upon my death I must confess. I have had ample time to consider my 57 years. I wish to leave this life and enter unto heaven unburdened from my sins. By now my story is well known tho the story oft told is a fallacy. My actions on the battlefield in 1775 do not represent the virtuous man I hoped I was. Twas my weapon that slay Bernadette Shaw. She hath no fault. Twas she that protected me after I took musket fire from the King's army. Tis her name that should adorn our town hall. In cowardice I stabbed her and claimed the spoils for myself. With this letter I set right the course of our township and country and restore the Shaw name. I leave you with an epitaph to mark her grave to atone, that which I have placed up at the site where her house once stood.*
>
> *With God as my witness, Rufus Burke*

Bernadette Shaw aged 30 years,
Behold all you that passeth by,
As you are now so once was I,
As I am now so you must be
Prepare for death and follow me.

The audience collectively exhaled. Emily Romero leaned into the microphone. "Thank you all for being here. It means a lot that you came to honor my sister. Like Bernadette Shaw, she was a protector until the end of her life. Like Bernadette Shaw, she was murdered for it. Having a room like this dedicated to her at the library is the type of thing Julie would love."

One person was missing from the crowd: Ms. Turlock.

Marion had called the police from Emily's house, right after she found the letter inside the incense box. They had found Ms. Turlock sitting in her chair in the school's main office, slowly spinning in circles, just waiting.

With the letter from Rufus Burke and the rest of the evidence Marion had gathered in her investigation, detectives had an easy time getting a confession from Jean Turlock. The game had taken its toll on her, and she'd never reaped any rewards. They had found Julie's remains where Ms. Turlock had left them in 1996, in a swampy area not far from the woods.

Emily continued, "Marion and Julie were the closest of friends. It's clear that they still are. Without Marion, Julie would still be missing. So please join me in thanking her for being here. I know you all want to hear her story of solving the case. Julie, always a lover of history and research, would be pleased."

Marion chronicled her investigation and with it her own transition from bystander to amateur investigator. No longer outside the action, Marion was the main event. She shared the key evidence and maps she'd made along the way, now displayed in the room as part of a permanent exhibit, then took questions from the crowd.

"Thank you for all your work, Marion. Why did Jean Turlock hide documents behind paintings?"

"Well, as we know now, this became a game to her. The Rufus Burke letter was the missing piece. She thought that by adding some mystery or intrigue and teasing us it might make us uncover that document. Obviously, Emily didn't figure it out right away—she had her picture hanging in her office for a couple of years. But I did. It was pretty easy to figure out that they were from Ms. Turlock. My documents included a letter that she'd signed, and Emily's had the Tang chart. It was Ms. Turlock's main thing: Tang—the thing that made her feel special, made students love her. It made her visible. Of course, I didn't know if her intentions were good or bad. The Ms. Turlock I knew wasn't a killer. It took more investigating to figure out she had that in her."

Another audience member raised a hand; Marion gestured, inviting him to speak.

"Why did Jean Turlock want the Rufus Burke letter so badly?"

"She saw an opportunity to blackmail the Burkes. When Julie had the letter, she asked Ms. Turlock about it. Probably just out of curiosity, because they were friends. Julie trusted her—we trusted her. Something clicked with Ms. Turlock, though. She got really interested and wanted it for herself. She was an outsider who had to witness the success and glory that came with being a Burke all day, every day for so many years. If she had the letter, she surmised, she might have a chance at money and recognition. She thought the Burkes might want to keep the letter hidden because it basically negated the founding history of the town and the basis for their fortune. Julie refused to hand it over; instead, she hid the letter in the incense box. And she was killed for it."

The questioner went on: "Was Robby trying to help when Jean shot him?"

Marion smiled. "Yeah, I got that wrong at first. I'll let him tell you." Marion gestured to Robby. He limped up to the podium. His leg was still healing.

"Thanks, Marion. Hi, everyone. Jean told me about Rufus and Bernadette Shaw about nine months ago. I'd never heard the story either. I began asking my family, trying to track things down. As far as I know, my living relatives didn't know about it. But Jean wouldn't quit. She followed me everywhere. Lurked in the shadows. Called at all hours. She was actually pretty scary, but I didn't really want to admit that everyone's favorite gentle old lady was freaking me out, so I tried to deal with it myself. I tried to suggest she retire. She kept saying she was owed more. I began to feel like she might be dangerous, so I tried to separate her and Marion. I didn't realize that Marion was doing her own investigation.

"Of course, I also didn't know if the stuff about Rufus was true or that Jean killed Julie. Obviously, now that this has all come to light we've begun to make reparations as a family."

Robby referred to the newly established Shaw Community Fund, governed by a cross-section of residents—the latest development in a string of changes the Burke family initiated once